Living an ENRICHED LIFE

Dale Carnegie Success Series titles published by Manjul Publishing House

- *Become an Effective Leader*
- *Communicating Your Way to Success*
- *10 Steps to a More Fulfilling Life*
- *How to Jump-Start Your (Next) Career*
- *How to Have Rewarding Relationships, Win Trust and Influence People*
- *Overcoming Worry & Stress*
- *Life Is Short Make It Great*
- *Embrace Change for Success*
- *Resolve Conflicts in Your Life*

Living an ENRICHED LIFE

DALE CARNEGIE

MANJUL
Manjul Publishing House

First published in India by

MANJUL

Manjul Publishing House

• 7/32, Ansari Road, Daryaganj, New Delhi 110 002 - India
Website: www.manjulindia.com

Registered Office:
• 10, Nishat Colony, Bhopal 462 003 - India

The Success Series:
Living an Enriched Life by *Dale Carnegie*

This edition first published in India in 2018

ISBN 978-93-87383-30-2

Cover Design by Trinankur Banerjee

Printed and bound in India by Thomson Press (India) Ltd.

CONTENTS

PREFACE

The longer I live, the more I realize the impact of attitude on life. Attitude to me is more important than facts. It is more important than the past, than education, than money, than circumstances, than failures, than appearance, giftedness or skill. It will make or break a company, a church, or a home. The remarkable thing is that we have a choice regarding the attitude we embrace for each day. We cannot change the inevitable. The only thing we can do is play on the one string we have, and that is ourselves. I am convinced that life is 10% what happens to me and 90% how I react to it. And so it is with you—we are in charge of our attitudes.

Dale Carnegie

Living an enriched life! Who would not want to get more out of the years they have on earth? We spend one-third of our lives asleep, at least one third working on our careers or taking care of our families and if we are lucky, the balance is created through recreational, cultural or religious pursuits or just through lolling around. Too many people live dull, drab lives, toiling in unsatisfying jobs, and using what free time they have in unrewarding pursuits.

In this book we will discuss some of the reasons we fall into these traps and provide some pointers to help overcome the problems and move forward to a better, more productive and more satisfying life.

Self-Confidence

The first matter to be discussed is Self-Confidence—the feeling we have about ourselves that we can accomplish anything we set out to do, is the essential element in living a full and meaningful life. The main reason many people never succeed in their jobs, their business ventures, and even in their personal lives is their lack of this key ingredient. Why do people lack self-confidence?

One common reason is that they have failed in some activity early in their lives and fear this will happen again. Another is that other people—their own parents, their teachers, their bosses—were never satisfied with their performance causing them to consider themselves failures.

Still others have tasted success only to have it followed by some sort of failure and have let that failure dominate their minds and doom them to a lack of self-confidence in anything they do. We will see how to overcome this and develop and maintain self-confidence along with a strong self-image.

Enthusiasm

A study of the lives of great men and women, whether they

are in government, business, science or the arts show that the one common trait all of them possess is enthusiasm about their work and their lives.

Enthusiasm is the secret ingredient of success as well as the generator of happiness in those people who possess it.

Enthusiasm makes the difference in one's attitude toward other people, toward one's job, and the world. It makes the big difference between a drab and an enriched life.

Setting and Achieving Goals

All successful people start with a goal. Establishing goals and working toward their achievement is the first step one must take on the long road to success. By knowing where we are going and how we plan to get there, we will be able to focus our time, energy and emotion, and start on the right track toward reaching those goals. We will study how to set goals that will inspire us to achieve high, how to assure that we do not deviate from those goals and how to overcome obstacles in reaching our goals.

Image

The image we project to people we meet is a major factor in the confidence they generate in us and whether or not they feel comfortable with us.

A pleasant, welcoming image can be *developed*. Some of the facets that make up our image are inborn—our physical appearance, basic intelligence and some talents—but each of us has the capacity to make the most of our innate traits and develop them to give us that type of image that others will admire.

It's not easy to grow into the person we want to be, but it starts with a strong desire and commitment to develop an outgoing, cheerful, optimistic and positive demeanor—an image that will win the approbation of the men and women with whom we interrelate.

We will learn how to make a good first impression, as well as how to maintain and improve that image.

Self-Motivation

Just wanting to accomplish our goals is not enough. We must constantly be cultivating the desire, the ambition, keeping those goals alive, being wholesome and healthy by active endeavor. This is the only way in which we can match our dreams with our realities. We will explore ways in which we can motivate ourselves to achieve our goals and learn techniques to move ourselves forward when we fall behind.

Be Positive

There is no uplifting habit better than that of bearing a hopeful attitude, of believing that things are going to turn out well and not ill; that we are going to succeed and not fail; that no matter what may or may not happen, we are going to be happy.

There is nothing else as helpful as the carrying on of this optimistic, expectant attitude—the attitude that always looks for and expects the best, the highest, the happiest—and never allowing oneself to get into a pessimistic, discouraging mood.

It is not always easy to remain positive, especially when matters do not go as we planned. We will learn how to overcome negativity and think affirmatively no matter what problems we face.

Be Courageous

Successful people have the courage to put their ideas into effect, the willingness to put their money, their efforts, their emotions into an enterprise in which they truly believe.

We must all take risks if we want to make progress in our jobs and in our lives. By careful analysis we can minimize the chances of failure, but we can never eliminate it. Without pain there is no gain. By always playing it safe, we may avoid that pain, but we will never feel the great joy and satisfaction that results from overcoming the obstacles and reaching our goals.

Bounce Back

Even when we have experience and know-how, we cannot always be successful. There will be times when we do fail, but we must not let the concept of failure overwhelm us. We learn from our mistakes and apply what we learn to overcome our failures.

Often disappointment or failure has a collateral consequence. It causes our morale to plummet and to destroy our self-confidence. Unless corrective action is taken immediately, this may deteriorate into self-pity, failure and unhappiness. We will explore how to deal with the psychological effects of defeats and restore our morale.

To get the most out of this book, first read all of it to absorb the overall concepts. Then reread each chapter and start applying the guidelines for achieving each of the areas covered. This will start you on the track to living an enriched life—a major step forward on the road to success.

—Arthur R. Pell, Ph.D.
Editor

1

BUILD UP SELF-CONFIDENCE

Believe in yourself! Have faith in your abilities! Without a humble but reasonable confidence in your own powers you cannot be successful or happy.

Dale Carnegie

When his company posted a position as a supervisor of a new department, Larry was tempted to apply, but after a moment he said to himself, "I'd like to move up, but I don't think I could handle it."

Susan made a suggestion to her boss for what she thought would improve productivity, but he pointed out several flaws in it. Susan's reaction: "I'm a failure. I just can't think things through. I'll never make another suggestion."

Claire was asked to chair a committee at her church. She told her husband: "I'd have to give talks to church members about this project. There's no way I could do that."

Eliot was the top salesman in his company for the first three months this year, but in the fourth month, he fell far behind. He said to himself: "I was lucky that first quarter, but the luck didn't hold and now I'm back where I belong—just barely meeting the quota. I knew it couldn't last."

What is the problem with these men and women? They all lack self-confidence. Each of them look upon themselves as basic failures, doomed to remain at the low end of the spectrum all of their lives.

There are times when any one of us may find ourselves doubting our abilities and our accomplishments and find our self-confidence plummeting. To make matters worse, we emphasize and dwell on what others think of us in order to determine how we feel about our abilities and ourselves. This mindset can lead us to avoid taking risks due to fear of failure.

Self-confidence is an integral part of self-esteem. Before we can gain the confidence in decisions we make, we must believe in ourselves. We must truly feel that we are someone of worth. If we do not have self-esteem, how can we be *confident* that our decisions are worthwhile?

Too often, we are more concerned about what others think of us than what we think about ourselves. William Becker, a mid-twentieth century clergyman and writer, admonished his readers: "Never mind what 'people' think of you. They may overestimate or underestimate you! Until they discover your real worth, your success depends mainly upon what you think of yourself and whether you believe in yourself. You can succeed if nobody else believes it, but you will never succeed if you don't believe in yourself."

The great Greek philosopher, Epicticus, said: "No man is free, who is not master of himself." Unless we have confidence in our abilities and faith and determination to succeed, we will never even get started on the road that leads to the achievement of our goals. We must expect great things from ourselves. This faith brings out the best that is in us. As the old saying states:

Life's battle does not always go
To the stronger or the faster man;
But soon or later, the man who wins
Is the one who THINKS he can.

We Are Who We (Not Others) Think We Are

People who are not self-confident put a lot of weight on what others think in order to determine how they feel about themselves. They avoid taking risks due to fear of failure and generally do not expect to be successful. They often put themselves down, discount positive feedback and subscribe to harmful assumptions that perpetuate self-defeating thought patterns and a negative attitude. Some self-defeating thought patterns include:

- Extreme Thinking: This is how Susan reacted to her boss's criticism of her suggestion. One failure led her to feel: "I am a total failure when my performance is not perfect."
- Imminent Disaster: Disaster lurks around every corner and becomes an expected outcome. For example, a single

negative detail, a bit of criticism, or a passing comment darkens all reality. "I blew that presentation and now I'll never get promoted."

- Magnification of the Negative: Good performance doesn't count nearly as much as bad performance—That was Eliot's reaction.

  "I know I had the best sales record the last quarter, but that was just luck. Now I'm back to my real self. I'm just making up to the quota this quarter."
- Overemphasis on "should" statements. "Should" statements are meant to push us toward the perfect scenario, but must be followed by a realistic thought process that establishes the "As is." Once these are established, we can plan on how to get from where we are to the "should be." Many times we just look at where we are and freeze with fear when we see we are not close to where we should be. This should, instead, be taken as a sign to stop, look and listen, so we could get on track.
- Being out of our comfort zones: From childhood on we develop an environment in which we are comfortable. In Sally's family, her father made all decisions. Children were told they were to be seen, but not heard. Today, as an adult, a wife, mother and employee, she is uncomfortable when asked to make decisions. Charlie spent many years as an administrative non-com in the US Army. He studied and followed the Army Regulations religiously. In his first civilian job after his retirement, he couldn't function efficiently because there were no equivalent written regulations in his company to guide him.

Sandra, the buyer of teen dresses for a local boutique was asked by her boss to narrate a fashion show, she was terrified. Speaking one to one to customers was routine and comfortable, but speaking to a group took her out of this comfort zone. Her boss suggested she take the Dale Carnegie Course to deal with this problem.

Dale Carnegie developed a method to help participants in his courses to overcome this discomfort by making each class member speak at least once in every class to an appreciative and encouraging audience. This has worked for thousands of participants in Dale Carnegie training programs, for over 90 years. It worked for Sandra, who now narrates fashion shows several times a year, and the compliments that she receives for her performance by her boss and her customers boosts her self-esteem.

Strategies for Developing Self-Confidence

The following strategies may help overcome self-defeating thought patterns:

Self-Acceptance

This comes from our ability to accept ourselves as human beings while focusing on our positive sides—our qualities, strengths, and traits—that make us who we are. When our focus is upon these areas of our self-image both confidence and self-esteem are positively influenced. It is all too common for people to focus upon their weaknesses instead of their strengths and therefore do more damage than good. We must help ourselves, and others to center on the positive pictures.

Focus on the Successes

The key here is to concentrate on our past success and achievements and to respect ourselves for the good we have done in the past. It is far easier to dwell on failures since others are only too eager to point them out to us. When we spend our time contemplating the many successes we have had in our lives, our perspective changes.

A valuable method of achieving this is to create an inventory of successes and accomplishments that we have had throughout our lives. At first it may be difficult to amass as complete a list as we would like but with persistence we can keep adding to our list and to our confidence.

Henrietta, a sales representative for a real estate firm in Orlando, Florida, received a letter from a client expressing her appreciation for helping her find her an "ideal home." Henrietta proudly showed it to everybody in the office. Her boss suggested that she set up a file in which she could place this letter and others she would get over time. He said, "This is your 'Success File.' These letters will cheer you up when things are not going great. They are evidence that you did it before and that you can do it again."

Henrietta followed his advice, but as every triumph she had was not substantiated with a letter, she added a "Success Log." In this log she listed her significant accomplishments—closing a tough sale, obtaining first sales rights for new homes from a major construction firm, making the most sales in the office for the month, etc.

All of us face slumps and down periods. Henrietta was no exception. When an "almost-sale" fell through, when faced with a dry spell, or when she just felt blue, she opened her "Success File," and reread those letters, reviewed the entries in her log. This restored her self-confidence and motivated her to get back to her real self.

Talk It Up

When we add the above two categories together and create a self-talk that is backed up by evidence, we will find that we have begin to believe the testimony. When a sports team is falling behind, the coach gives it a pep talk. We are our own coach, so we must give ourselves that pep talk. What do we say? We create an argument that would hold up to scrutiny due to the weight of the evidence. The stronger and more compelling the evidence is, the more believable and powerful the message. It is an internal discussion we must all have from time to time. This is a tool to take back control of the only thing over which we have ultimate control all the time—our thinking. In other words, we must psych ourselves to restore our self-confidence.

After Henrietta reviewed her success file, she created a self-talk based on the evidence in that file. She repeated it over and over again to herself and just as those coaches motivated their teams she motivated herself to renewed successes.

> *By talking to yourself every hour of the day, you can direct your thoughts towards those of courage and happiness, of power and peace. By talking to yourself about the things you have to be grateful for, you can fill your mind with thoughts that soar and sing.*
>
> *Dale Carnegie*

Know What You Want and How You'll Achieve It

1. Concentrate on the goal you want to attain. It is not sufficient merely to say: "I want a job with good potential." Be definite. "I want a job as a marketing researcher with opportunity to prove that I can move into management."
2. Create a definite plan for carrying out your desire, and begin at once—whether you are ready or not—to put this plan into action.
3. Write out a clear, concise statement of your objective and what you intend to do in order to achieve it.
4. Read this written statement aloud, twice daily, once just before retiring at night, and once after arising in the morning. As you read, you must see and feel and believe you are already achieving the goal.

Self-Confident People Take Risks

Approach new experiences as opportunities to learn rather than challenges to win or lose. Doing so opens one up to new possibilities and can increase your sense of self-acceptance. Not doing so turns every possibility into an opportunity for failure, and inhibits personal growth.

Some people never take risks. They always play it safe. Most likely they will always be just average, mediocre performers. They will never have any real success. By not taking the chance that something they supported might not work out, they avoid the "agony of defeat," but never experience "the thrill of victory."

The turtle is a living fortress. Its impervious shell protects it from all harm. However, if the turtle wants to move, it must stick its head and neck out from the shell, exposing itself to the dangers of the environment. Like the turtle, if we want to move ahead we cannot surround ourselves with perfect protection. We have to stick out our necks in order to progress.

Taking risks does not mean one must be a daredevil. Reasonable people take reasonable risks, but by definition, a risk may not succeed. Successful business executives take risks with every decision they make. However, they maximize their chance of success by careful research and analysis before making the decision. But when that decision finally has to be made, the manager must be willing to risk the possible loss of money, time, energy and emotion. Without risk, there is no possibility of gain.

It is the end of the ninth inning. The Red Sox lead the Yankees 2 to 1. The first two hitters strike out. Dave Winfield, the Yankee's ace hitter is at bat. The ball comes straight across the plate. Wham! a clean hit. Winfield races to first. He makes it easily. Should he try for a double?

In microseconds, Dave must decide if he should play it safe or take the risk of trying for that extra base which would put him in a scoring position. If he fails, the game is over, but by taking a chance he increases the possibility of turning defeat into victory. Winfield is a risk taker and if there's only a slightly better than even chance of success, he tried for the double. Champions have self-confidence. In life as well as in sports they will take chances. That is what makes them champions.

In his book *How to Stop Worrying and Start Living*, Dale Carnegie advises that when facing trouble: "Ask yourself: 'What is the worst that can possibly happen? then prepare to accept the worst; try to improve on the worst.'"

These principles can be applied in determining whether or not to take a chance on an innovative, radical or just different approach to a problem.

Gil Baker had not been able to obtain an appointment with Stan Green, the purchasing manager of a prospective customer. He had phoned, written letters and even "sat on his doorstep"—all to no avail. His colleagues advised him to forget Green and use his energies and time to develop other leads. But Gil was stubborn. There must be some way to get Green's attention. He learned that Green was to be a speaker at an industry workshop. "If I attend the workshop," thought Gil, "I can approach him after his talk, ask him some questions and then identify myself, so he'll at least know who I am."

His sales managers and co-workers discouraged this. "He'll be so mad that he never will speak to anybody from this company again."

Gil responded by applying Carnegie's principles. "What is the worst that could happen? He won't do business with us. That's not so bad because he isn't doing business with us now, so we have nothing to lose."

'Prepare to accept the worst: If I do not make an impression on him at the meeting, I'll give up working on that account."

"Try to improve on the worst: By carefully planning the questions I ask, I can demonstrate that I am truly knowledgeable about his business and this may overcome his reluctance to see me."

By taking a chance, Gil reached an "unreachable" prospect and opened a very profitable account for his company.

We must all take risks if we want to make progress in our jobs and in our lives. By careful analysis we can minimize the chances of failure, but we can never eliminate it. By always playing it safe, we may avoid that pain, but we will never feel the great joy and satisfaction that results from overcoming the obstacles and reaching our goals.

Aggressive versus Assertive

There is a difference between being a self-confident and assertive person and being an arbitrary and aggressive person. Most people appreciate boldness and confidence as long as it is not communicated with insensitivity. Many of the personal and corporate success stories that we know are the result of an individual or group of individuals assertively pressing on. Yet, there seems to be a lot of misconceptions about assertiveness versus aggressiveness or passivity. Assertive behavior has been defined as "... standing up for yourself in such a way that it does not violate the basic rights of another person."

The fundamental difference between assertiveness and aggressiveness is most often a self-esteem issue. Dale Carnegie's human relations principles teaches us to strike the balance. Instead of "walking over people" or "being walked on by people," it provides a way of "walking with people" to achieve a win-win result. Assertive communication is a human relations approach that combines strength and sensitivity.

The following chart (Figure 1) illustrates the difference between an assertive self-confident approach and an aggressive one:

Figure 1: Aggressive versus Assertive versus Passive

Aggressive	Assertive	Passive
Self-centered	Will stand up for their own rights while being sensitive to others	Concerned about others to the point of personal detriment
Often is stressed and stresses others	Deals with stressful situation and moves on.	Stressed internally though may not show
Often manifested as a result of poor self-esteem	Requires a strong self-image	Often manifested as a result of poor self-esteem
Direct to the point of inappropriateness	Direct, honest, appropriate communication	Indirect and often not to self
May not be liked or respected Puts down others	Often respected by others Builds others up	Often liked, but may not be respected Builds others up even at his own expense
Feels a need to control everything and everyone; holds others accountable but not themselves	Willing to take personal responsibility for their own actions	Holds themselves accountable, but not others
Confrontive—forces others to follow Restrictive	Tends to lead by example, does not seek nor avoid confrontations; Flexible with guidelines	Avoids confrontation—often overly apologetic; Strict guidelines for self, but not for others

Vocally abrasive	Open, yet sensitive, polite	Reserved, indirect, restrained
Extremely direct—forces thoughts, ideas on others	Direct but considerate	Avoids expressing feelings
Demands	Asks	Wishes

Help Others Achieve Self-Esteem

As parents, we can build self-confidence and self-esteem in our children. As managers, we can build self-confidence and self-esteem in our staffs. As teachers or coaches, we can build self-confidence and self-esteem in our students or teams. Teach them to believe in themselves. Give them the opportunity to express themselves.

Harvey Mackey, founder and CEO of Mackey Envelope Co., and author of many books on self-improvement, said in an interview in *Personal Excellence:*

> *Finally, it's important to give everyone a sense of being significant. In a bad environment, everyone feels like a victim. In a good one, people feel as if they have equal worth—perhaps not equal power, but equal worth. A production line worker may not be able to enforce his desires in the same way a senior executive can, but the production line worker has an equal chance to be heard, in the same way that the youngest child gets equal air time at the dinner table.*

What this all adds up to is one loud, clear message—you're special, and we care about you. For your child and your employee to succeed individually and the entire family or organization to thrive, each has to care about the other.

Sum and Substance

- Never allow yourself to think meanly, narrowly, poorly of yourself. Never regard yourself as weak, inefficient, diseased, but as perfect, complete, whole.
- Never even think of the possibility of going through life as a failure or a partial failure.
- Stoutly assert that there is a place for you in the world, and that you are going to fill it.
- Train yourself to expect great things of yourself. Never admit even by your manner that you think you are destined to do little things all your life. If you practice and persistently hold the positive, producing, opulent thought, this mental attitude will some day make a place for you, and create that which you desire.

2

BECOME TRULY ENTHUSIASTIC

Enthusiasm is the dynamic of your personality. Without it, whatever abilities you may possess lie dormant; and it is safe to say that nearly every man has more latent power than he ever learns to use. You may have knowledge, sound judgment, good reasoning facilities; but no one—not even yourself—will know it until you discover how to put your heart into thought and action.

Dale Carnegie

If there is one ingredient of success that surpasses all others, it is enthusiasm. Enthusiasm is an inner excitement that permeates the whole being. The word comes from two Greek roots: *en* meaning "in" and *theos* meaning "God."

Literally, the person with enthusiasm has God within. It is an inner glow—an ardent, spiritual quality deep inside a person.

An enthusiastic attitude is fundamental to self-fulfillment. It guides us towards positive thoughts and actions. It creates positive energy that improves our relationships with others, our willingness to be open to new ideas, and even our health. The reverse is also true. Dale Carnegie wrote that our fatigue is often caused not by work, but by worry, frustration and resentment.

Enthusiasm for life initiates within us the power to change our lives. Focus on the present to nourish that power. Enthusiasm for life facilitates our ability to release regrets about the past and worries concerning the future. We can't change the past, we can influence future outcomes with a positive, enthusiastic approach to the opportunities of the present.

When our thoughts are propelled by an enthusiasm for life, we find we have unlimited power to develop our own unique potential whether it be in business, sports, community life or family. In time, guilt, fear and worry are replaced by confidence and optimism.

Dale Carnegie wrote; "Remember, happiness doesn't depend on who you are or what you have; it depends solely on what you think. So start each day by thinking of all the things you have to be thankful for. Your future will depend very largely on the thoughts you think today. So think thoughts of hope and confidence and love and success."

Psychologists report that IQ tests have one important shortcoming. They fail to measure the "emotional drive"—the psychological term for enthusiasm. According to IQ tests, a person with a low score is usually rated as fit for only menial jobs, whereas a high score is considered practically a guarantee of success. This, we know is misleading. We have seen people with low IQ's suddenly "set on fire" by a new idea or a new line of work. It created within them the enthusiasm that leads them on to great success. We have also witnessed the opposite—very intelligent men and women who do not succeed in their lives.

When Mark Twain was asked the reason for his success, he replied: "I was born excited."

In his book, *The Excitement of Teaching,* William Lyon Phelps, a Yale University professor wrote: "With me, teaching is more than an art or an occupation—it is a passion. I love to teach, as a painter loves to paint, as a singer loves to sing, as a poet loves to write. Before I get out of bed in the morning, I think with ardent delight of my first group of students."

One of the chief reasons for success in life is the ability to maintain a daily interest in one's work, to have a chronic enthusiasm; to regard each day as important.'

Enthusiasm Leads to Action

Development of enthusiasm in individuals, groups, athletic teams, companies and total communities pays off in positive action—in success and happiness. This can be observed in athletic competitions. Norman Vincent Peale, one of Dale Carnegie's friends and colleagues tells the story of Vince Lombardi, one of the greatest football coaches of all time. When Lombardi was chosen to coach the Green Bay Packers (an American football team), he faced a defeated, dispirited team. He stood before them, looked over them silently for a long time and then in a quiet, but intense voice said: "Gentlemen, we are going to have a great football team. We are going to win games. Get that. You are going to learn to block. You are going to learn to run. You are going to learn to tackle. You are going to outplay the teams that come against you. Get that."

"And how is this to be done? You are to have confidence in me and enthusiasm for my system. The secret of the whole matter is what goes up on here (and he tapped his temple). Hereafter, I want you to think of only three things: your home, your religion, and the Green Bay Packers, in that order. Let enthusiasm take hold of you."

The men sat up straight in their chairs. "I walked out of that meeting," wrote the quarterback, "feeling ten feet tall."

That year the Packers won seven games—with virtually the same players that had lost ten games the year before. The next year they won the division title, and the third year, the world championship. Why? Because, added to hard work and skill and love of the sport, enthusiasm made the difference.

Dale Carnegie often quoted Frederick Williamson, one-time president of the New York Central Railroad:

"The longer I live, the more certain I am that that enthusiasm is the little-recognized secret of success. The difference in actual skill, ability, and intelligence between those who succeed and those who fail is usually not very great. But if two men are about equally matched, the man who is enthusiastic will often outstrip one who has first-rate ability, but no enthusiasm."

When Sir Edward Victor Appleton, who had been awarded the Nobel Prize in physics, was made Chancellor of the University of Edinburgh, *TIME* magazine sent him a cable asking him if he had any recipe for success. "Yes," he replied, "enthusiasm. I rate that even ahead of professional skill."

Thomas A. Edison said: "When a man dies, if he can pass enthusiasm along to his children, he has left them an estate of incalculable value." Experience proves that to be true. It is more than wealth, for enthusiasm will produce not only wealth but also a great zest for living.

Enthusiasm Comes From Within

Enthusiasm is not skin-deep. It must emanate from within a person. It rarely can be feigned for a sustained period of time. One way of generating a continued surge of enthusiasm is to set a goal and work toward it, and when it is accomplished set another goal and work toward it. The excitement and challenge it provides cannot help but keep one enthusiastic.

When feeling blue, some people sing to themselves to overcome their sadness. By acting happy they restore their happiness. The same principle applies to enthusiasm. If we stimulate animation and excitement for our work or other facets of our lives, we will usually find that we've stimulated ourselves right into the middle of the kind of emotional drive we are seeking.

> *How can you make yourself become enthusiastic? By telling yourself what you like about what you are doing and pass on quickly from the part you don't like to the part you do like. Then act enthusiastic; tell someone about it; let them know why it interests you.*
>
> *Dale Carnegie*

Find Something to Become Enthusiastic About

Do not confuse enthusiasm with noise, shouting or yelling. Dale Carnegie defines enthusiasm as an ardent spiritual quality deep inside—a suppressed excitement. He says: "If your heart is on fire with a desire to help others, you will be excited. Your excitement will radiate through your eyes, your face, your soul and your whole personality. You will be inspired and your inspiration will inspire others." To be truly excited about something, we must feel that passion deep inside ourselves. However, we are often required to do things about which we do not have that deep commitment. One way that helps develop enthusiasm is to find something in the assignment about which we can become excited. By focusing on this, real enthusiasm will be generated.

Carol had her first job as a junior associate after graduating from law school. She dreaded the time-consuming and dull work of researching cases in the law library, but unless this was done, the case her firm was trying could not be properly prepared. What would be the benefit to her from doing this necessary, but boring job? Carol realized that this was a test of her capability as a new lawyer in the firm. By concentrating on how finding details important to the case would reflect on her career, she became enthusiastic about seeking out these details and became truly enthusiastic about the assignment.

Become an Expert in the Subject

Learn as much as possible about the subject. Learning leads to knowledge and often engenders excitement about the matters learned.

When Andy was hired to be the assistant to the Town Supervisor, he expected to be involved in working on solving many of the political problems faced in the township. However, his boss assigned him to very routine work, such as checking on whether forms were filled out properly, assuring that documents were properly processed and handling similar detail work.

After a few months, he complained to the Town Supervisor, "The work you give me could be done by a high school drop-out. I'm a college grad and can be much more valuable to the office if you would give me higher level work." The Supervisor responded: "Andy, I hired you because I know you can be a great help to me in important matters, but understanding the basics of what we do here will give you the foundation needed to take on additional responsibilities. Rather than looking at these assignments as boring clerical details, study what they represent, why the details are needed and how they relate to the smooth operation of our office."

Andy took his advice. Instead of just checking for accuracy, he studied the material, asked questions about it and learned as much as he could about the process that ensued in resolving each issue. It was not long before he started looking forward to each day and to what new things he would learn.

> *The way to acquire enthusiasm is to believe in what you are doing and in yourself and to want to get something definite accomplished. Enthusiasm will follow as night follows the day.*
>
> *Dale Carnegie*

Try a Different Approach

Alfred M. represents a company that leases cranes to contractors in South Africa. He reported on how he applied the concept of enthusiasm to opening one of the toughest accounts in his industry.

The customer, whom he called "Mr. Smith," was always rude and usually in a violent temper. After two calls in which Smith refused to listen to his presentation, Alfred was about to give up, but he resolved not to lose his enthusiasm and to try once again.

Through the open door from the waiting room to Smith's office, Alfred could see him ranting and raving at another salesman. He almost physically pushed him out of the office and shouted: "Next!"

In Alfred's words: I walked into his office. He shouted, "You again—I told you 'no' already. Why are you bothering me?" Before he could say anything else, I smiled and without the tremor most salesmen had in their voice when addressing him, I said in my most enthusiastic manner. "I want all of your crane hire business."

He stood there behind his desk for about fifteen seconds, speechless. He looked at me in an odd way and said: "You sit there and wait for me," and left the room. When he returned a half hour later, he looked at me quizzically and snarled, "Why are you still here?" I told him that I had such a good deal for him that I wouldn't think of leaving until I could explain it to him. The result was an order amounting to 75,000 rands per month for a year's contract, with good possibilities for more business.

Self-Talk

In the previous chapter we discussed how giving oneself a pep talk is an effective way to gain self-confidence. It also works as a tool to engender enthusiasm for what we are doing.

Lisa's goal was to become a medical secretary. She completed the course required and set out to find a job. After several rejections due to her lack of experience, she became discouraged. When she went to her next interview, she paused before entering the building. "What's the use? I'll run into the same thing again." Instead of giving up, Lisa gave herself a pep talk. "I want this job and I have the technical know-how. I was the topper of my class in the school. I am a diligent and conscientious worker. I can do this job and will be a real asset to the doctor. She repeated this over and over again in her head as she waited for the doctor to see her. Her enthusiasm manifested itself in the answers to his questions and she was offered the job.

Some months later the doctor told her that when he saw from her application that she had no work experience, he had decided to give her just a courtesy interview and reject her. But he was so impressed by her enthusiasm, it convinced him to hire her. She carried that enthusiasm into the work itself and became a very successful medical secretary.

> *Enthusiasm is not merely an outward expression. It works from within. Enthusiasm is born of a genuine liking for what you are doing.*
>
> *Dale Carnegie*

Enthusiasm Can Overcome Adversity

Andrew Grove is a man whose triumph over adversity was fueled by his great enthusiasm. A native of Hungary, he had first been persecuted by the Nazis during World War II, and later by the Russians when they invaded Hungary in 1956.

He fled to America when he was 20 years old with only a few dollars in his pocket, and only a little knowledge of English. Despite many hardships he never lost his enthusiasm for obtaining knowledge and making a success of his life. By working any job he could find, he put himself through New York's City College, earning a Bachelor of Science degree in Chemical Engineering. He received his masters and Ph.D. from the University of California at Berkeley.

Andrew Grove has played perhaps the pivotal role in the development and popularization of the 20th Century's most remarkable innovation—the personal computer. The technologies pioneered by Grove and his associates, first at Fairchild Semiconductor and then at Intel, which he co-founded in 1968, made the entire personal computing revolution possible. The world has barely begun to scratch the surface of the technological and economic benefits that such revolution can bring.

He was no stranger to problems and setbacks, but he always managed to retain his enthusiasm and maintain his focus on what is important and what he does best: developing even faster, more affordable and more powerful technology.

Thanks to Andrew Grove's genius and vision, millions of people now have instant and inexpensive access to the kinds of information and entertainment about which even the elites of previous generations could only dream. In 1997, Andrew Grove was chosen by TIME magazine as their person of the year. A few years ago Grove learned that he had prostate cancer. He determined to fight it with the same energy and enthusiasm that he used to build Intel. As of now he is winning the battle.

Grove has shown us that opportunity for success and wealth is not restricted by adversity, persecution or poverty. By vision, enthusiasm and hard work, one can make the vision a reality and great things can be accomplished. Set backs—whether they are business problems or serious diseases—can be overcome if we have the enthusiasm to deal with them.

Dale Carnegie was so impressed by the following poem by the 19th century American philosopher, Samuel Ullman, that he had a plaque quoting it hung over his desk:

You are as young as your faith,
As old as your doubts;
As young as your self-confidence
As old as your fears;
As young as your hope,
As old as your despair.
Years may wrinkle the skin,
But to give up enthusiasm
Wrinkles the soul.

Attitude

A prerequisite for becoming an enthusiastic and self-motivated person is believing that things are going to turn out well and not ill; that we are going to succeed and not fail; that no matter what may or may not happen, we are going to be happy.

There is nothing else so helpful as the carrying of this optimistic, expectant attitude—the attitude that always looks for and expects the best, the highest, the happiest—and never allowing oneself to get into a pessimistic, discouraged mood.

We must believe that we will do what we were made to do. Never for an instant must we harbor a doubt of it. It does not matter what we are trying to do or to be, we should always assume an expectant, hopeful, optimistic attitude regarding it. It will enable us to grow in all our faculties.

Successful people treat themselves properly by encouraging themselves and by making their minds positive, to will be immune from all negative, discouraging thoughts.

The only world we will ever know anything about, the only world that is true for us at this moment, is the one we create mentally—the world we are conscious of. The environment we fashion out of our thoughts, our beliefs, our ideals, our philosophy is the only one we will ever live in. Another inspiration, new ideas will come tomorrow. Today we should carry out the inspiration of the day.

No human being has succeeded in trying to be somebody else, even if that person was a success. Success cannot be copied—cannot be successfully imitated. It is an original force—an individual creation.

Enthusiasm comes from within or from nowhere. We must be ourselves. We must listen to the voice within. There is room for improvement in every profession, in every trade, and in every business. The world wants people who can do things in new and better ways. Don't think that because your plan or idea has no precedent, or because you are young and inexperienced, that you will not get a hearing. People who have anything new and valuable to give to the world will be heard and will be followed. People who dare to think their own thoughts and originate their own methods, who are not afraid to be themselves, and are not a copy of someone else, gets recognition quickly. Nothing else will attract the attention of an employer or the rest of the world so quickly as originality and unique ways of doing things, especially if they are effective.

Control Your Thoughts

Considering that our mind governs everything in our world, its force has been singularly neglected and misunderstood.

Even when tribute is paid to its power, it is treated as something unalterable, a tool that could be used if one was born with the genius to do so. Of recent years, the control of thought, and its use to modify character already formed, to change even external surroundings, or at least their effect on one's self, and to bring about health, happiness, and success, is increasingly being studied and understood.

A strong man hypnotized into a belief that he cannot rise from his chair is actually powerless to do so until the spell is removed. A frail woman, nerved by necessity to save a life, can carry a person heavier than herself from during by fire or flood. In both cases the mental attitude, not the physical ability, determines the result; yet both acts are only work of muscles.

When a task to be done consists largely or wholly of mental acts, as most achievements, how much greater must be the determining power of the thought. The conquerors of the world, whether on battlefields, in trade or in moral struggles, have won by the attitude of mind with which they went to their work.

There is no certainty in the presence of doubt. Until we erase "fate" and "can't" and "doubt" from our vocabulary, we cannot rise. We cannot get strong while we harbor convictions of weakness, or be happy while we dwell on miseries or misfortunes

There's no way we can become well and strong by always thinking and talking about our bad health, saying that we never expect to be robust or well. Neither can we expect our executive faculties to be strong and vigorous while we perpetually doubt our ability to do what we undertake. Nothing so weakens the mind and renders it totally unfit for effective thinking as the constant acknowledgment of weakness, or doubt of one's ability to accomplish a task.

There can be no more important study, no higher duty owed to ourselves than that of thought-control and of self-control, which results in self-development. Perhaps because thought in itself is intangible, and most of us really have so little control over it, there is an impression that direction of mind action is a difficult and abstruse affair, something that requires hard study, leisure, and book knowledge to accomplish it. Nothing is further from the truth. All of us have within ourselves all that is required to remake our intellectual nature, our character, and resultantly, change our lives for the better.

Channel Enthusiasm Into Action

Self-confidence enables us to be enthusiastic about our activities and to accomplish results by eliminating fear, doubt, and uncertainty. The mind cannot act with vigor in the presence of doubt. There must be certainty, or there would be no efficiency.

We must concentrate on our goal, see before us the prize as though it were already won, while being intensely conscious of moving nearer to its achievement. This will generate the enthusiasm that helps us on our way. One by one obstacles vanish, and what once seemed too hard for human strength to accomplish appear plain and even simple. The greatest need of all is to keep the goal in sight and not let interest flag or inward vision waver.

Enthusiasm alone will not accomplish results. Outward work must follow inward contemplation. Wishes alone will not absolve us from the need of making effort, but it is a means for revealing to us what efforts we need to make and how to make them.

Ten Techniques Proven to Engender Enthusiasm:

1. Adopt a definite major purpose—that aspect of our job or our life in which we want to become more enthusiastic. Write out a clear statement of that purpose and our plan for attaining it.

   When Harry was elected chairman of the fund raising drive for his community center, his goal was to generate as much enthusiasm as he had about the project in other members of the committee and in turn the entire membership of the organization. He carefully thought out his plan of action, published it in the organization bulletin and had copies emailed to the entire committee. Now everybody involved was made aware of his plan and how he or she could help achieve it. But more importantly, he made large-print copies of it, and posted them on his bathroom mirror, on the refrigerator in his kitchen and on the wall next to his desk to keep himself notified and refreshed on his plan and to maintain his enthusiasm for it.

2. Attack the plan with a burning desire to make it work. Never let your enthusiasm for it fade. Think about it every day and every night. Let it become the dominating thought in your minds.
3. Don't procrastinate. Set to work immediately in carrying out your plan. Harry met with his committee and together they drew up an action program indicating who would do what, timetables, and expected results.
4. Set up procedures for follow-up. Too often the best-laid plans are nothing more than words because nobody checks progress. When what is planned does not happen, the enthusiasm of the start-up begins to fade. Harry set checkpoints so that each member could measure his or her own activities.
5. Setbacks and snags are most likely to occur. There are people who lose their enthusiasm if things don't go well. This is when your enthusiasm will act as an adrenaline shot and give others the energy to fight and correct it. It may be necessary to change direction—but not necessarily. Evaluate what went wrong. It may just require minor adjustments, but if serious problems developed, re-examine what occurred. However, if you find that you are significantly off track, it may be necessary to rethink the plan and rewrite it. By maintaining you enthusiasm, you could approach the problem not as an unpleasant chore, but as an exciting opportunity.

6. You are not alone. Just like an athletic team has its cheerleaders, you need a "cheer squad" to applaud you when you succeed and to boost you up when you are behind. However, unlike the college cheer leader, you should select men and women who are not only positive thinkers, but have knowledge and experience that can help you in your endeavors.

   Harry had a mentor, who had guided him in his career and never failed to encourage him when things were not going well. With the help of his mentor, he assembled a group of people who had previous experience in fund raising to guide over the rough spots.
7. Beware of pessimists. The world is filled with naysayers—men and women who always predict failure. They doom every effort and when setbacks do occur, instead of helping they say: "I told you so." Keep these people off your committee or team. If you are compelled to work with such people, you should surround yourself with optimists who can counteract their negativity.
8. Make a habit of being enthusiastic. Habits require reinforcement. Never let a day pass without devoting some time to furthering the plan.
9. Never give up on the idea that you will achieve your goal, no matter how far away that moment seems. When enthusiasm is waning, an "internal pep talk" will reinforce it.
10. Be positive at all times. Enthusiasm thrives on hope, confidence, selflessness, assurance and tolerance. Maintain that positive attitude and your project assuredly will move forward.

Ralph Waldo Emerson, who is considered the greatest of American philosophers, saw the value of enthusiasm. In one of his essays he wrote: "Every great and commanding moment in the annals of the world is the triumph of some enthusiasm."

Sum and Substance

- Enthusiasm is the little-recognized secret of success.
- Set a goal and work toward it, and when it is accomplished set another goal and work toward it. The excitement and challenge it provides cannot help but keep one enthusiastic.
- Study the subject. Learning leads to knowledge that leads to enthusiasm about the matters learned.
- By far the men and women who are most enthusiastic are those who are self-motivated. We are our own best motivators. If we believe in ourselves and in our inevitable success, we create within ourselves a never-ending source of enthusiasm.
- Always assume an expectant, hopeful, optimistic attitude. It will generate enthusiasm for whatever we are engaged in.
- Faith in ourselves enables us to be enthusiastic about our activities and to accomplish results by eliminating fear, doubt, and uncertainty. The mind cannot act with vigor in the presence of doubt. There must be certainty, or there would be no efficiency.
- Never give up on the idea that we will achieve our goal, no matter how far away that moment seems. An "internal pep-talk" will help when enthusiasm begins to wane.

3

SET AND REACH ACHIEVABLE GOALS

All successful people start with a goal. Establishing goals and working toward their achievement is the first step one must take on the long road to success. By knowing where we are going and how we plan to get there, we will be able to focus our time, energy and emotion—and start on the right track toward reaching those goals.

A ship, which has broken its rudder, may keep everlastingly at it, may keep on a full head of steam, sailing around all the time, but never arrives anywhere. It never reaches any port unless by accident; and if it does find a haven, its cargo may not be suited to the people, the climate or the conditions. The ship must be directed to a definite port, for which its cargo is adapted, and where there is a demand for it, and it must aim steadily for that port through sunshine and storm, through tempest and fog.

So a person who wants to succeed must not drift about rudderless on the ocean of life, but must not only steer straight toward a destined port when the ocean is smooth, when the currents and winds serve, but also must keep the course in the very teeth of the wind and tempest, and even when enveloped in the fogs of disappointment and mists of opposition.

It Starts with a Dream

We start with a dream—a vision of the future. In the dream we are rich, famous and happy. Most people do dream of such a future, but in most cases, that's all it will ever be—a dream.

Successful people have had those dreams too, but they turned those dreams into goals and in turn into reality. But their dreams were not vague hopes for success, but dreams of specific achievements that they aimed for. Edison dreamed of a world in which electric energy would light up the night. Gates dreamed of a computer system that would enable everybody—not just big organizations—to utilize the power of computers. Beethoven dreamed of music that would make the spirit soar. Great actors, artists, musicians, writers dreamed, not just of fame but of the way they would utilize their talents to achieve success.

Dreaming is not limited to such geniuses. All successful people report that their success started with a hope, a dream. Men and women who have been queried about their achievements reported over and over again that it all started with a dream, which led to a goal, which led to a plan of action and inevitably to accomplishing the goal.

Dreaming is not limited to the young. It is never too late to have a new dream that leads to new goals that in turn leads to new successes. It is astonishing what people who have had their dreams late in life have accomplished. Benjamin Franklin was past fifty before he began the study of science and philosophy. Milton, in his blindness, was past the age of fifty when he sat down to complete his epic poem—*Paradise Lost*.

Dreaming is not limited to biases and prejudices of the times. For countless years, women have been restricted in what they can attempt to accomplish. Their career goals were limited to what were considered "female jobs." It took determination and courage to even think about other careers. One example is Elaine Pagels, Princeton professor and best-selling author of books on Gnosticism and early Christianity. She said she was educated at a time when girls were taught to not even consider serious careers. She felt free to follow what she loved; only later discovering she could make a living out of it. Her dream had become her goal.

> *Are you doing the work you like best? If not, do something about it. You will never achieve real success unless you like what you are doing. Many people have had to try several things before they knew what they wanted to do.*
>
> *Dale Carnegie*

Today the barriers are gone in most career areas. For example, in most law, medical and other professional schools in the United States, half or more of the students are women.

In the nineteenth century, Frederick Douglas, born into slavery, did not let his race or condition of servitude stop him from learning to read and write and eventually to become a leader of his people. In the twenty-first century, Barack Obama broke the race barrier to become president of the United States.

Even brains are second in importance to will. Vacillators are always pushed aside in the race of life. Only those with an iron will and determination that nothing shall impede them, are sure that with perseverance and grit, they will succeed. Dreams become goals and goals become achievements to those who strive long enough and hard enough.

Most of the things which make life worth living, which have emancipated us from drudgery and lifted us above commonness and ugliness—the great amenities of life—we owe to our dreamers.

Converting Dreams Into Goals

Unfortunately, too many dreamers remain just that—dreamers. The dreams remain dreams. When we convert dreams into goals, they are no longer fantasies, but objectives that we can set before us as a road map to success. We must bring to our dreams a purpose, a determination that we will do all that we can to make that dream come true.

A woman who had a dream and converted it into a successful goal is the clothes designer, Rachel Roy. Rachel's love for fashion was inspired by the movies she saw as a child. The clothes the women on the screen wore seemed to give them an aura of confidence and success. Rachel dreamed that she could create the same aura for herself and other women—a sophisticated look that would create positive self-esteem.

She and her family went school shopping once a year. She was disturbed by the lack of interesting clothing choices in a local store and was convinced that if she had the opportunity she could create better styles. Her mother told her that this was the job of a buyer. Now she could put a name to her dream: buyer. At that moment, she said, her dream became her goal—to become a buyer in the fashion field.

Her first job was as stock clerk. She moved rapidly to assistant manager, to personal shopper, to stylist in various stores. She was soon designing fashions and was on the road to a senior position in her company.

When her husband, Damon Dash, wanted to start an independent clothing line, Rachel had a decision to make—to leave her own successful career and start over with Damon. She chose to start over, throwing herself into the job, working in every capacity, tracking everything she did to contribute, and involving herself in as many facets of the business as possible. She wanted to make herself irreplaceable. After about six years, Rachel was confident she could run a business herself and formed her own company. Her designs were acclaimed by the industry and today she is considered one of the foremost designers in the fashion industry.

There is an infinite distance between the wishers and the doers. Rachel Roy was more than a dreamer and a wisher. She turned her dream into a goal and worked hard to achieve that goal.

The very habit of expecting that the future is full of good things for you, that you are going to be prosperous and happy, that you are going to have a fine family, a beautiful home, a successful career, and are going to stand for something, is the best kind of capital on which to start your life.

What we try persistently is what we tend to achieve, even though it may not seem likely or even possible. If we always try to express the ideal, and we visualize it as vividly as possible and try with all our might to realize it, it is more likely we will achieve those things we would like to come true in our lives, whether it be robust health, a noble character, or a superb career. It is only when desire crystallizes into resolve that it is effective. It is the desire coupled with the vigorous determination to realize it that produces the creative power. It is the yearning, the longing, and striving together that produce results.

If we wish to improve ourselves in any particular area, we must visualize the quality as vividly and as tenaciously as possible, and hold a superior ideal along the line of our ambition. We must keep this persistently in the mind until we feel its uplift and realization in our lives. We are born to win, to conquer and to lead a triumphant lives. We should be a success in our chosen work, our relationship with people, and in all other phases of our lives.

Believe, and Achieve

Prosperity begins in the mind and is impossible while the mental attitude is hostile to it. It is fatal to work for one thing and to expect something else, because everything must be created mentally first and is bound to follow its mental pattern.

We cannot become prosperous if we really expect or half expect to remain poor. We tend to get what we expect, and to expect nothing is to get nothing.

When every step we take is on the road to failure, how can we hope to arrive at success? It is about facing the wrong way toward the black, depressing, hopeless outlook, even though we may be working in the opposite direction that kills the results of our effort.

Thoughts are magnets that attract things like themselves.

If your mind dwells upon poverty and disease, it will bring poverty and disease. There is no possibility of producing just the opposite of what we are holding in our minds, because our mental attitude is the pattern, which is built into our lives. Our accomplishments are achieved mentally first.

The terror of failure, the fear of financial loss and of possible humiliation keep multitudes of people from obtaining the very things they desire.

The habit of looking at everything constructively, from the bright, hopeful side, the side of faith and assurance, instead of from the side of doubt and uncertainty; and the habit of believing the best is going to happen, that the right must triumph; the faith that truth is bound finally to conquer error; that harmony and health are the reality and discord and disease the temporary absence of it—this is the attitude of an optimist, which will ultimately reform the world.

Setting the Stage for Success

We cannot depend on others to set us on the road to success. It depends entirely on ourselves.

Before we can determine what goals can get us started on this journey, we must first evaluate ourselves. We must search deep inside of our minds and pull out from it what it is we really want out of life and what assets we have that will lead us to reach that goal.

We must be realistic. We may want to establish a goal that appears to be desirable, but we may not have the abilities needed to achieve it. We may dream of being a movie star or an opera singer, but don't have the talent needed. Our dream career may be in areas that are not feasible for us to attempt.

On the other hand, we may have aptitudes and skills that we don't realize we have and which can lead to a satisfying and profitable career.

How can we find out? By looking deep inside ourselves. A careful introspection will bring this out. Most adults already know what they can and cannot do, what they like and do not like. It may not be obvious, but introspection enables us to go beyond the obvious and think deeply about ourselves.

A good example of this is Shonda Rhimes, creator and executive producer of the television shows "Grey's Anatomy" and "Private Practice." Even as a child she knew that she would become a creative writer. She made up stories and spoke them into a tape recorder before she knew how to write. Her mother encouraged her by transcribing them, hence making them real.

What we have to do is go systematically over our education, previous experience, hobbies and interests. Look for those aspects of our lives in which we have been successful and in which we have achieved satisfaction and joy. These are indicators of the areas in which we will succeed in the future. But this is only the beginning. Look beyond what we *have* accomplished and think what we *can* accomplish.

Successful people learn at the very outset of their careers just what funds they can draw upon. We must take an inventory of all our possible assets and resources. Let's not just look at what we have accomplished so far in our lives, but what we know we can accomplish. The great majority of young people start on their careers with little knowledge of their mental capacities and they usually discover them piece by piece over time.

Too many people never discover more than a small

percent of their ability and rarely rise above low paid, low-level positions. They plod along in mediocrity; yet they have resources, if they could only detect them, it could lift them into superior positions.

Somehow they never come in touch with just the right kind of ambition-arousing material, ambition-arousing environment or the necessary material to ignite the giant power of their hidden strengths.

Oneness of Purpose

Successful people strongly believe that one must be totally committed to one's goals. There is great power in a resolution that has no reservation in it—a strong, persistent, tenacious purpose which burns all bridges behind it, clears all obstacles from its path, and arrives at its goal, no matter how long it may take, no matter what the sacrifice or the cost.

To succeed we must concentrate all the faculties of our minds upon one unwavering aim, and have the tenacity of purpose, which leads to defeat or victory. Every other inclination that tempts us must be suppressed.

Developing goals that are reasonable and achievable is the first step to success—whether it is in our career or any other aspect of our lives. We must plant the seeds in our minds that will enable us to accept and implement these goals.

Establishing Goals

Peter M. always knew he wanted to be an engineer. As a child his primary interests were mechanical. In school he excelled in math and science. His career goals were solid and he followed them through college and into the world of work.

Most of us are not that fortunate. We only have vague concepts of careers as a child and often "fall into" our careers by fortuity. However, it is never too late to establish goals—not only in our job and career but also in other aspects of our life.

Elvira S. floundered through several jobs after college. She had majored in marketing, but her first job in that field bored her to tears. She shifted to sales, but was unhappy and unsuccessful. Her next job, a paralegal in a law firm, really excited her and created in her an interest in becoming an attorney.

She set a new long-term goal—to become a criminal lawyer. She requested transfer within her firm to work for their senior attorney who handled criminal matters. She attended law school at night and received her law degree shortly. Further, she set a goal to work in the office of the District Attorney to gain experience before starting her own practice.

> *If you've been unsuccessful in something you've wanted very much to do, don't give up and accept defeat. Try something else. You have more than one string for your bow—if only you discover that string.*
>
> *Dale Carnegie*

Guidelines For Setting Goals

To make goals more than just pipe dreams, they should combine the following elements:

- *Goals should be clearly stated*: Indicate in clear terms what you wish to accomplish. Be specific and firm in stating the goal. For example, saying "My goal is to be the best salesperson in my company" sounds good, but it is better to be more specific: "My goal is to reach a sales volume of so many dollars for the next fiscal year; and ten percent more each year for the next three years." Now you know the target and your subconscious mind will help concentrate your efforts on reaching those figures.

- *Reasonable*: Unless the goals set can be attained, setting goal is meaningless. To assure reasonableness, break the long-term goal into attainable sub-goals. For example, Long-term goal: exhibit my paintings in a prestigious art gallery in next three years. Intermediate goals: To complete X canvasses by December of next year; to mount a showing at a local art gallery by July of the following year; to be reviewed in an art journal by December of that year.
- *Goals should be inspiring:* If we set a goal that is too easily attained, it will not motivate us to do more than minimum work. We should set goals that will inspire us to keep moving ahead and to work much harder to achieve them. Achievers recognize that once a goal is reached, they should immediately set another goal that will make them stretch themselves to continue to improve and grow.
- *Goals should be action based:* Unless the actions that will be taken to implement the goals are noted, the goals are no more than dreams. Action requires activity—mental, physical, and emotional. Mentally, we must be prepared to think about our goals every spare moment and what actions must be taken to realize them.
- *Goals should be measurable:* It is not always possible to quantify goals. Some goals can be measured in financial or other numerical terms. We can set sales figures that we wish to attain by the month, quarter, or year—in terms of units

of product or dollar value. We can set production goals by amount. Even intangible goals, which cannot be quantified, can be established in measurable terms. The major goal can be broken into segments and timetables set for the completion of each segment. In this way we can measure how close we are in reaching each of the segments and fine-tune our activities to assure that they will be accomplished in a timely manner.

- *Goals should be written down:* One way to assure that goals will not be forgotten or lost in our hectic day-to-day lives is to write them down. Make a list of long-term goals; break them into intermediate and short-term goals. Write them in large letters and post them where you can see them every day—over your desk, on the refrigerator, on the mirror. Read them, memorize them, re-read them and ask each day: "What am I doing to accomplish these goals?"
- *Goals should be flexible:* There are times when circumstances change and the goal we set is no longer pertinent. Economic conditions may not be favorable for starting that new enterprise; technological innovations may have made the goal obsolete; we may have made errors in our research and the goal is not feasible. This does not necessarily mean the goal must be abandoned. It may just require new thinking or more study. If faced with such a situation, review what has transpired and make necessary adjustments.

  One often fails to meet a set goal. Don't become frustrated and give up. Review what has transpired, evaluate the situation and make necessary adjustments.

  Hugh had expected that he would be promoted to store manager after serving two years as assistant manager. It didn't happen. Rather than quitting in frustration, Hugh reviewed the situation. His company had opened six to ten new stores each year for the past six years and he had based his goal on the premise that his company would continue to open several new stores each year. Last year business had not been good and they had only opened two new outlets. But this year business had improved and he knew that additional openings were being considered. By adjusting his goals, he extended his timetable for another year and will most likely reach it.

- *Goals should be stretched:* Once you have reached a goal, set another that will make you stretch in order to continue to improve and grow. When Ben started his physical fitness program he was told that if he swam thirty laps in half an hour, he would keep in good shape. It didn't take him long to achieve that goal. Most people of his age—the late fifties—would have been content to keep swimming at that pace, but Ben learned that in the 25-yards pool that he used, 36 laps was equal to one-half mile. He immediately strove to reach that new goal.
- *Let others know our goals:* In most weight-loss programs, participants are advised to let their families know how much weight they intend to lose and keep them reminded of their progress. Why? When we share our goal with others, they will support us in helping reach it. When we are tempted to give up, they encourage us to continue.

Karen had dropped out of college when she got married, so she could work until her husband completed his education. Then she planned to return and get her degree. The birth of her children changed this plan. Now, ten years, later, Karen managed to resume her education. Managing a house, working an eight-hour day and going to school at night is tough. From time to time, Karen feels it's not worth the effort. But because her husband, children and friends know how important that goal is to her, they cheer her on and encourage her to keep going.

- *Review progress:* All goals cannot be quantified so that they can be easily measured, but when this is possible, set specific standards and timetables. When not quantifiable, develop a way of measuring how close you have come to attain your goals.

  When Lee set his sales goals for the year, he expected to increase his annual volume by eight percent. This meant he would have to open at least four new accounts or increase the sales of his current customers. He broke this down into monthly goals that could be easily measured against his actual sales. If business did not measure up to the monthly goal, he could take necessary steps immediately to get back on track.

  As Human Resources Director of her organization, Kathy could not set quantifiable goals. Her objectives for the next twelve months included setting up a new training program for word processor operators, studying and reporting to management on a new type of benefits package, and designing a performance review system for administrative and professional personnel.

  She broke each of these objectives into segments and set timetables for each segment. In this way she measured how close she was to reaching each of the segments and fine-tune her activities to assure she would accomplish all of them by the end of the year.

We all have possibilities we don't know about. We can do things we don't even dream we can do.

Dale Carnegie

The Planning Process

A systematic approach to establish goals for a specific project should follow the following steps:

Step 1. Should-Be

This is the scope of the project. It is a picture of what you ultimately want, and who and how it would be beneficial. This should be clearly stated and agreed upon among senior managers, your team and yourself. If you have not done a good job of defining scope, planning the project will be almost impossible.

Step 2. As-Is

Examine the current situation. Where are you today? What factors help or hinder your efforts to carry out the project scope?

Step 3. Goals

Now you are ready to define and set realistic goals to successfully carry out the scope of the project. Without such goals, one tends to drift. Goals can be immediate, intermediate, or long-term. Achieving day-to-day goals (immediate goals) contribute to the achievement of intermediate and long-term goals. Review what constitutes a SMART goal:

- S = Specific in terms of processes and resources
- M = Measurable by objective data
- A = Attainable in that they can be achieved
- R = Relevant to your vision
- T = Time specific with a deadline

Step 4. Action Steps

In order to achieve goals, priorities must be established and specific action steps must be developed. In order for goals to be met, action steps should include:

- Requirements of the job
- Who will do the job
- Methods to be used
- How the different parts tie together and fit into the big picture
- How you want the results communicated (report, PowerPoint, etc.)

Step 5. Cost

Another aspect to planning is determining the budget for, and cost of, each action step. Costs include that of personnel, equipment, material and any other costs required to achieve the goal.

Step 6. Timetables

Deadlines should be set and communicated so there is a clear understanding of immediate, intermediate, and long-term targets to be met. When establishing timetables, be realistic. Work backward to determine when each phase should be completed. Put the schedule in writing to avoid misunderstandings.

Step 7. Implementation

An important yet overlooked part of implementing a plan is making sure that everybody involved understand their role in achieving the goals. Commitment to agreed-upon results must be established. Monitoring the implementation may result in modifying the scope of the plan and re-evaluation goals.

Step 8. Follow-Up/Measurement

A critical part of the planning process is to keep accurate records, analyze why deviations have occurred, and take action to correct any challenges. Concentrate on those factors critical to reaching the goal.

By establishing a well-thought out goal standard, you would be able to focus on your true objectives, measure your progress and assure that what is most important to you in your job or other aspects of your life be accomplished.

Sum and Substance

- All successful people report that their success started with a hope, a dream, which led to a goal, which led to a plan of action and inevitably, to accomplishing the goal.
- Before you can determine what goals can get you started on the journey, you must first evaluate yourself. You must search deep inside your mind and determine what it is that you really want out of your life and what assets you have that will help you in reaching that goal.

- Developing goals that are reasonable and achievable is the first step to success.
- Follow these guidelines for setting goals:
  Goals should be clearly stated.
  Goals should be reasonably attainable.
  Goals should be inspiring.
  Goals should be action based.
  Goals should be measurable.
  Goals should be written down.
  Goals should be flexible.
  Goals should be stretched.
  Goals should be shared with others who can support you.
  Goals should be reviewed periodically to measure progress.

4

HOW OTHERS SEE US

The old adage: "You can't judge a book by its cover," makes good sense but unfortunately, most of us do judge people by their "cover"—their appearance and demeanor at the first meeting. Indeed, some people make a decision about an individual in the first thirty seconds of contact.

First impressions are hard to overcome. If a negative or undesirable impression is made on that first contact, it may permeate all relations with that party for years to come. It takes a little thought and effort to establish the basis for making good impressions, but it is well worth the effort.

Create an Image of Success

When we meet successful people, we are often impressed by their pleasant personality. The image that we receive makes us confide in them, admire them, and feel comfortable with them. Sometimes we meet unpleasant people and are repelled by the image they project.

Our image—sometimes called our personality—is the way in which we express ourselves to the outside world. We are not only gregarious animals, liking to be in the sight of other people, but we have an innate propensity to get ourselves noticed, and noticed favorably. Much of this image comes from a fine, cultivated manner. Tact is a very important element, next only to fine manner—perhaps the most important. One must know exactly what to do, and be able to do just the right thing at the proper time. Good judgment and common sense are indispensable to those who are trying to develop a positive image.

One of the greatest investments one can make is that of attaining a gracious manner, cordiality of bearing, generosity of feeling—the delightful art of pleasing. It is infinitely better than money or capital, for all doors fly open to sunny, pleasing personalities. They are more than welcome; they are sought out for everywhere.

Personality Traits Can Be Acquired

Assuming that all people have equal rights and opportunities, we must recognize that all do not have equal intelligence, equal physical strength, equal levels of energy; yet whatever their status, they may rise by self-education and self-development. Those eager for knowledge, ambitious to excel, will naturally forge ahead. Consequently, we can choose and work to develop the personality traits we wish to acquire. Application is the great thing.

The important thing to remember is that a pleasant, welcoming image can be *developed.* Although some facets that make up our image are inborn—our physical appearance, basic intelligence and some talents—each of us has the capacity to make the most of our innate traits and to develop them to give us a type of image that others will admire.

It's not easy to grow into the person we want to be, but it starts with a strong desire and commitment to develop an outgoing, cheerful, optimistic, and positive demeanor—an image that will win the approbation of the men and women with whom we interrelate.

Maintain a Cheerful Disposition

Unless we have a mental attitude that is free of bitterness and guile and we look at each day as a blessing to be enjoyed and savored, we will have an unhappy and most likely unproductive life.

Some people harbor for years a bitter hatred or a great jealousy toward others. Although they may not be aware of it, such a mental attitude does not allow the possessors to reach the highest levels of their abilities, and destroy their happiness.

Moreover, they radiate their destructive energy thus prejudicing people against them, arousing their antagonism, and constantly handicapping themselves all along the line.

The mind must be kept free from bitterness, jealousy, hatred, envy, and uncharitable thoughts; free from everything which inhibits it, or there must be a penalty paid in terms of impaired efficiency, inferior work as well as loss of peace of mind.

We cannot do our best work while we harbor revengeful

or even unfriendly thoughts toward others. Our faculties only give up their best when working in perfect harmony. There must be good will in the heart or we will be incapable of doing good work. Hatred, revenge, and jealousy are poisons, fatal to all that is noblest in us, as arsenic is fatal to physical life.

A kindly attitude, a feeling of good will toward others is our best protection against bitter hatred or injurious thoughts of any kind. It will lead to a life of peace and equanimity. It will minimize discord in our lives and help us maintain harmonious relations with others.

We cannot carry secret hatreds and grudges, jealousies, and revengeful feelings without seriously impairing our own reputation. Many people wonder why they are not popular, why they are disliked generally, why they stand for so little in their community, when it is really because of their bitter, revengeful, discordant feelings, which kill personal magnetism.

On the other hand, if we maintain kind, loving, helpful sympathetic thoughts, feel friendly toward everybody, and carry no bitterness, hatred, or jealousy in our hearts, we will create an attractive, helpful, and sunny image.

> *Flaming enthusiasm, backed up by horse sense and persistence, is the quality that most frequently makes for success.*
>
> *Dale Carnegie*

People who can smile when things go wrong have a tremendous advantage over those whose courage collapses just as soon as they are in a hard place. People who can smile when everything seems to go against them will always project the image that they are made of winning material.

First Things First

When people meet us, the first factor that makes an impression on them is how we look. Appearance plays a major part in how we are perceived. Some of the factors that may impress others either positively or negatively are beyond our control. We cannot change our basic physical appearance, but we can make the most of our assets and minimize what may be perceived to be defects. One does not have to have movie-star good looks to make a positive impression.

The Critical Ten Seconds

Each time a new person meets us, that person takes just ten seconds to form a whole laundry list of impressions, beliefs or assumptions regarding who we are and what we are about.

And those assumptions are far more significant than how much we paid for our clothes and whether or not that's our natural hair color. Those impressions encompass everything from our education level to our financial situation, our career success, even things as subjective as our honesty and integrity. All those beliefs are formed, almost subconsciously, in the first ten seconds.

External Image

Our external image is what others observe first. It can be an effective door opener or a door closer. Every salesperson knows the frustration of not being able to get to a prospect because he can't get past the so-called "gatekeeper"—the receptionist, secretary, or subordinate who screens out unwanted callers. In a sense, a person's first impression of us is the most powerful gatekeeper of all. It often determines whether that person would let us in, figuratively as well as literally.

The bulk of the cues to our external image are transmitted visually. The newest brain research reveals that visual impulses are transmitted directly to the emotional center of the brain, bypassing the normal routing systems and forming responses almost instantaneously.

Good grooming, appropriate dress, a pleasant smile, and proper manners are the first steps in making a good personal impression. We can maximize our chances of success by dressing in a way that communicates a positive message about us and our abilities.

With the widespread adoption of business casual dress codes, there is no one right way to dress for business today. We must do some research to find what is appropriate in our industry, region, and culture.

The day before Phyllis was scheduled to be interviewed by the ABC Ad Agency, she went to the lobby of their building and observed how the women who worked there dressed. She noted that unlike the bank where she had formerly been employed, most women wore blouses and skirts or slacks—not dresses. So when she went for her interview, she dressed accordingly. Had she worn one of the outfits she had worn in the bank, she would not have presented an image of somebody who would fit into that environment. On the other hand, had she applied to another bank, dressing in casual attire would have made a poor impression.

Be Interested in Others

> *Remember that the person you are talking to is a hundred times more interested in himself and his wants and his problems than he is in you and your problems.*
>
> *Dale Carnegie*

Appearance and personality are only the first step in creating and maintaining the image others have of us. We must develop it by becoming, as Dale Carnegie said, "genuinely interested in other people."

If we make a point of showing sincere interest in somebody from the moment of initial contact, it will work more than anything else to develop instant rapport. We must make the effort to note that person's name and use it when addressing him or her.

In a business situation, listen intently to the problem or situation that the person has come to discuss and ask questions that show you are genuinely concerned. In social situations, show sincere interest when responding to the other person's comments and questions.

Alfred Adler, the famous Viennese psychologist said in his book *What Life Should Mean to You,* "It is the individual who is not interested in his fellow men who has the greatest difficulties in life and provides the greatest injury to others. It is from among such individuals that all human failures spring."

One of the characteristics that made Theodore Roosevelt one of the best-liked people of his time was the sincere interest he showed in every person he met. He would ask them about their families and listen to their ideas—no matter how humble their backgrounds. He took the time to get to know each of the members of the household staff of the White House and even years after he left office, when he visited the White House, he greeted each by name and commented about an interest that they had expressed or something they had done for him when he was the president. How could anybody keep from liking him?

If you want to make friends, greet people with animation and enthusiasm. When somebody calls you on the telephone, say "hello" in a tone that lets him or her know how pleased you are to receive the call. Showing a genuine interest in others not only wins friends, but also helps develop customers' loyalty to your company.

It was often said about Daniel Webster, the great orator and statesman that he gained the trust of every person he met. When asked why people had such an immediate reaction to him, they commented that unlike most politicians, he listened to what they had to say about themselves rather than talk about himself.

Be empathetic. Empathetic people put themselves in the shoes of the people with whom they interact. They not only hear what other's have to say, but feel what they feel when they say it.

First Impression on the Telephone

Often the first contact we have with somebody is on the telephone. The future relationships one would have with that person can be established by the impression one makes in this phone call. Jennifer was upset. The washing machine she had purchased only last month had broken down. She called the store and asked for the manager. After six rings, the call was answered: "Jones' Appliances, Please wait." She waited and waited and waited for what appeared to be an eternity. Just as Jennifer was about to hang up and dial again, the operator finally came back on the line:

"Jones' Appliances, can I help you?"

"May I please speak to the manager?"

"What for?"

"I bought a washer last month and it broke down."

"You don't want the manager, I'll connect you with service."

After another long wait, the service representative finally responded. Half way through Jennifer's complaint, he interrupted: "Sorry, we can't help you. You have to go to the manufacturer. You'll find the address on your warranty," and without waiting for a response hung up.

Do you think Jennifer will ever buy anything from that store again?

To make a good impression on callers, answer the telephone promptly. If you know that the person will have to wait for any length of time, let that person know approximately how long and suggest that you would be happy to call them back. In case the individual elects to wait, have somebody advise them that you are still looking into the problem, so they have the option of either continuing to wait or request that the call be returned.

When speaking with the caller, always let them talk until the complaint or message is fully explained. Do not interrupt. If you cannot help, give as much information as you can to enable the person to obtain the help needed.

Our Workplace Creates First Impressions

Gary's eyes scanned the room. It was certainly a busy office. People were scurrying back and forth; the desks he could see were piled with papers. Phones rang, and nobody answered. The one word that popped into Gary's head was "chaos." He began to have reservations about doing business with this organization. When he finally met with the company's representative, this first impression had predetermined his decision.

The company Gary visited might have been highly competent to handle Gary's business, but by not paying enough attention to the little things that add up to the impression made on visitors, everything that followed was almost automatically rejected.

When visitors enter the place of business, whether they are customers, bankers, potential employees, or government regulators, the impression made by the first sight influences the manner in which they perceive the company.

Obviously, a machine shop cannot be as spotless as a doctor's office, but it should at least be as neat as other machine shops.

It's a good idea for people to check their facility periodically to assure that it is clean and orderly; that tools and equipments are properly stored when not used; that desks are not overflowing with papers; and in general, that there is a business like atmosphere.

Correspondence Creates First Impressions

When Warren attended a time management seminar, he was told that the time spent on writing business letters could be shortened significantly if the writer would just jot down the response on the bottom of the letter received and mail it back to the person who sent it. Warren put this idea into practice immediately. It certainly did save time, but in doing this, the image of his company suffered.

In following up a sales lead that he had answered in this matter, he learned that the prospect decided not to do business with Warren's company because their response to his inquiry was "unprofessional."

Our correspondence represents us to the public. Our letterhead should be designed to represent the image we wish to present. Spelling and typographical errors can be interpreted as indicators of a careless or inefficient operation. Intelligent readers readily detect poor choice of words or incorrect grammar. Reread correspondence before mailing. Make sure all letters are error-free.

Nonverbal Communication

Some of the routine behaviors we exhibit on autopilot can be strengthened to help us communicate positive messages about ourselves to those with whom we interact. These superficial behaviors have an enormous impact on the impressions we make.

Sociolinguist Albert Mehrabian, in his exhaustive study of face-to-face communication, determined that only 7 percent of the message transferred from one person to the other was housed in spoken words. About 38 percent of the meanings were transmitted through vocal characteristics—tone of voice, pauses, emphasis, etc. And an astonishing 55 percent of the total message was communicated through visual signals we classify as "body language."

The famous presidential debates between the young John F. Kennedy and the much more experienced Richard Nixon are a classic example. Radio listeners who only received the verbal portion of the message felt that Nixon excelled, but millions of viewers who saw the additional nonverbal component on television had exactly the opposite impression. Nixon's facial expressions, his sweating and hand movements made a negative impression on the viewer.

Posture

Good (or bad) posture is seen even from a distance, and registers instantly in the viewer's brain. It is less subtle than other nonverbal cues because it involves the entire body.

In research projects, participants assumed that subjects with excellent posture were more popular, ambitious, confidant, friendly, and intelligent than others with a more relaxed stance.

Improving our posture may feel awkward and exaggerated at first. By observing the impact of an upright torso, squared shoulders, and balanced lower body in other people, we can see how impressive they look, and learn how to look equally impressive.

Using Our Head

The position of our head and the movements of our features play a significant role in nonverbal communication. We should keep a level head to make the maximum impression.

Of all facial expressions, the smile is the most influential. Smiling can actually cause others to be more receptive to our point of view. When we smile, the other person nearly always smiles back. More than just a mirroring, it reflects the sudden surge of warmth and well-being that our smile generates.

However, an insincere smile is more damaging than no smile. A believable smile uses the entire face and happens spontaneously when we process a positive thought about the interchange we are a part of.

Eye Contact

Effective eye contact implies confidence, honesty, and interest in the other person. Lack of eye contact is usually interpreted as a sign of fear, dishonesty, hostility, or boredom.

Research shows that in job interviews candidates give more complete and revealing answers when the interviewer maintains eye contact. In classes, student comprehension and retention of the materials are directly related to the instructor's eye contact.

Handshakes

In America and Europe, the handshake is a significant part of the introduction when meeting new people. An effective handshake communicates an unconscious but important message to others about our self-esteem, energy, and enthusiasm. A handshake also creates a personal connection that makes the other party more open and honest.

Feedback

Perhaps the most challenging aspect of managing our external image is the difficulty of seeing ourselves as others see us. Research indicates that we are probably more critical of ourselves than others are of us. And at the same time, we may be totally unaware of negative behaviors that need to be corrected.

Some ways to get an accurate view of our own external image include:

- Seeing and listening to ourselves on videotape
- Studying our mirror image as we speak
- Asking trusted colleagues for honest input
- Monitoring others' reactions to us—especially those whom we want to influence

Building an Impressive Image

When we describe someone with an effective executive image, we nearly always describe an individual with high credibility. Others can count on such a person's words and their ability to make positive things happen.

When we choose a new behavior and then follow through on that commitment, we build credibility with our most important audience—ourselves. We prove to ourselves that we have the personal power to overcome our reluctance and make things happen.

Our attitudes are intimately intertwined with our actions. It is virtually impossible to maintain a change in one without a change in the other. There is no "quick-fix" to shortcut, but each instance of taking positive action adds another link to the chain that holds up our executive image.

To help track your successes, think of one important professional goal—something that really matters to you—perhaps something you have been putting off or feeling reluctant to tackle.

Then take one step, however small, that will move you toward that goal. Analyze what has been done so far and what it accomplished. If you feel confident that it has been achieved, select another step, and so on until you reach the image you want.

Of course some of the shortcomings we see in ourselves need to be corrected, rather than accepted. By identifying and filtering out misconceptions that we may have about our weak points releases energy to work constructively on strengthening those weak areas.

Benjamin Franklin, in his autobiography, describes his fruitless attempts over the years to rid himself of numerous negative behaviors. However, he found great success when he decided to focus on a single behavior until he had eliminated it from his life; then he moved on to tackle another behavior.

> *Instead of worrying about what people say of you, why not spend time trying to accomplish something they will admire.*
>
> *Dale Carnegie*

Internal Image

Trying to create a positive image with others without first building a firm foundation of self-awareness and self-confidence is the equivalent of using Band-Aids when we need antibiotics. It is an attempt to treat surface symptoms rather than creating overall good health.

Interpersonal effectiveness rests on sharing ourselves with others, and it is simply too threatening for most of us to share openly until we have a high level of comfort with our own identity. We cannot give others the acceptance they desperately need unless we first give that same acceptance to ourselves.

You may have been advised to adhere to the concept of "fake it till you make it?" That can be an excellent strategy in the short term. When you face a new situation and feel the almost inevitable butterflies despite your inner belief in your resources—take a deep breath and dive in. And just like a dip in a swimming pool, your ability and energy will pull you to the top.

However, unless your self-confidence is solidly in place, you can't fool all the people all the time. So why bother trying? Instead, you should invest your time and energy in re-establishing a strong sense of personal value and ability.

Assurance can be nurtured in a variety of ways. One important tool for revitalizing our sense of self-confidence is a review of past accomplishments. One way of doing this is to keep a success file as discussed in Chapter 1 of this book. Reviewing your past successes is a sure way of reinforcing your self-image.

Maintaining a positive attitude is important in every area of executive image, but nowhere is it more critical than in our attitude toward ourselves. Most of us—even the most seemingly successful—carry around a mental suitcase full of negative messages about ourselves. They may have come from parents, teachers, bosses, colleagues, or even our own imagination, but we have the capacity to recolor those messages and make positive beliefs our conscious choice. How to overcome negativism and maintain a more positive self-image will be discussed in Chapter 6.

We can control the image we present to others by creating within ourselves the internal image that will radiate from us to the outside world. The time and effort we devote to developing a positive, warm, welcoming image will result in our acceptance by others and strengthen the relationships we develop in our business and social lives.

Sum and Substance

- A person's first impression of us is the most powerful gatekeeper of all. It often determines whether that person will let us in, figuratively as well as literally.
- Maintaining a positive attitude is important in every area of executive image, but nowhere is it more critical than in our attitude toward ourselves.
- One of the greatest investments one can make is that of attaining a gracious manner, cordiality of bearing, generosity of feeling—the delightful art of pleasing.
- To make a good impression on telephone callers, answer the telephone promptly. While speaking with the caller, always let them talk until the complaint or message is fully explained. Do not interrupt. If you cannot help, give as much information as you can to enable the person to obtain the help needed.
- We should take a look at our facility with the eyes of a stranger. Ensure that the place of business reflects an image of professionalism.
- Our correspondence represents us to the public. Spelling and typographical errors can be interpreted as indicators of a careless or inefficient operation. Reread correspondence before mailing. Make sure all letters are error-free.
- Try to see yourself as others see you. Make an effort to identify and correct negative behaviors.
- Unless you have a mental attitude that is free of negativity

and look at each day as a blessing to be enjoyed and savored, you will have an unhappy and most likely unproductive life.

- You can improve our external image if you follow Dale Carnegie's principles of dealing with others:
  1. Don't criticize, condemn, or complain.
  2. Give honest, sincere appreciation.
  3. Arouse in the other person an eager want.
  4. Become genuinely interested in other people.
  5. Smile.
  6. Remember that a person's name is to that person the sweetest sound in any language.
  7. Be a good listener. Encourage others to talk about themselves.
  8. Talk in terms of the other person's interests.
  9. Make the other person feel important—and do it sincerely.

5

WE ARE OUR OWN BEST MOTIVATOR

There is no better uplifting habit than that of bearing a hopeful attitude, of believing that things are going to turn out well and not ill; that we are going to succeed and not fail; that no matter what may or may not happen, we are going to be happy. But unfortunately, there are times when we may dim our chances for success at the very outset by expecting that we are going to fail, thinking that the chances are against us. In other words, if our mental attitude is not favorable to the success that we are after, it could sometimes even attract failure. Success is achieved mentally first. If the mental attitude is one of doubt, the results will correspond. This is the time when we must motivate ourselves to overcome these doubts and move on to success.

When we begin to doubt ourselves, when we feel things are not going right, we must give ourselves a pep talk. We must say—and say it out loud—that we are going to succeed. There is a force in spoken word that is not stirred by going over the same mentally. When we hear them they make a more lasting impression upon the mind. We know we are more powerfully impressed and inspired by listening to a great lecture or sermon than if we read the same thing in print. We remember the spoken word even when we forget the cold print that is carried to the brain. It makes a deeper impression on the inner self.

> *By talking to yourself every hour of the day, you can direct yourself to think thoughts of courage and happiness, thoughts of power and peace. By talking to yourself about the things you have to be grateful for, you can fill your mind with thoughts that soar and sing.*
>
> *Dale Carnegie*

We must visualize ourselves as achieving our goals. Follow the lead of successful people—think only of success. It is our responsibility to keep ourselves motivated.

What Do We Mean By Motivation

Let's look carefully at this word. Another word beginning with the first three letters M-O-T that's related to motivation is MOTION. Motivation involves putting one into motion—getting one to get up and *do* something. Another word that begins with the letters M-O-T is MOTOR. The great automobile pioneer, R.E. Olds remarked that he likens a person to an automobile. He reminds us that the propelling power in a car is its motor—its internal combustion engine. Each of us has a motor inside of us—an engine that is combusting internally to keep us in motion.

Just as the engine in the car requires fuel to make it go, we also require fuel to make us go. Just as all auto engines do not use the same kind of fuel—some cars use gasoline, some electric batteries, some steam—the same fuel does not motivate all people. Some people's motivation is fueled by a desire to make money; some to gain fame; some to create great art or music; some to perfect an invention; some to gain happiness and satisfaction.

Who will provide the fuel to motivate us? It may come from an employer who compliments us for exceptional production. It may come from awards given by universities, foundations or governments. It may come from the profits of a company we created or manage. It may come from a variety of outside sources. But by far the men and women who are highly motivated to succeed provide their own fuel. The best motivator is within our own minds. If we believe in ourselves and in our inevitable success, we create within ourselves a never-ending source of fuel to put and keep us in motion.

We must concentrate our efforts in order to marshal the forces within us to continually fuel us to be self-motivated. It starts with our attitude. We must stimulate our mind and our body to put out the extra effort needed to succeed. We must have faith in ourselves and in our goals to provide the foundation to sustain our motivation. This will be the foundation on which we will conquer obstacles and disappointments.

We Can Make It Happen

The reason why so many people fail to realize their ideals is because they are not willing to do their part to make it real. Remember that the longing, the desire to do a certain thing, is merely sowing the seed of our ambition. If we stop at this we will get about as much harvest as the farmer would get if he put his seed in the ground without preparing the soil, without fertilizing it, and keeping the weeds down.

We must back up that which our heart longs to realize with an honest purpose to do our best, and a dead-in-earnest effort to make our vision real.

The mere holding of desire to do so, no matter how persistently or strongly we hold it, will not help us to realize our dreams. We must not only sow the seed of desire and longing, but we must also do all the nourishing, cultivating, caring for, or we will only reap a harvest of weeds. We see men and women everywhere reaping a weedy harvest from the sowing of mere longings. These people can scarcely get enough out of their harvest to keep them alive, simply because they took no care of their seed after the planting.

The constant nursing, cultivating the desire, the ambition, keeping our heart's longings and soul's yearnings alive, wholesome and healthy by actively working to achieve them, is the only way in which we can match our dreams with our realities.

The framework of our life structure is invisible. It is on the mental plane. We are laying the foundation for our future, fixing its limits by the expectations we are visualizing. We cannot do anything bigger than we plan to do. The mental plans always come first. Our future building will merely be carrying out in detail what we are visualizing today. The future is simply an extension of the present. Our thought habit, our prevailing mental attitude determines our place in life. We are locating ourselves, settling what we are to be. It will be broad, ever growing, ever expanding, or it will become narrower, more restricted and stolid, according to our mental plan, and according to the vision we maintain.

Successful people, without knowing it, encourage themselves by making their minds positive, so that they could be immune from all negative, discouraging thoughts. Holding the thought of success, the prosperity ideal, constantly dwelling upon one's successful future, expecting it, working for it—these are, whether we know it or not, success, or prosperity treatments.

Stay Focused

Dave Thomas, born and raised in poverty, never lost faith in himself. He created the Wendy's Restaurant chain and built it into one of the most successful fast-food chains in the United States.

When he was asked about what he believed was important to his success, he responded:

"Stay focused on meeting your goals. Don't be distracted by trying to accomplish too many things at the same time. Without a doubt, motivation is a key to success. You must keep in mind what motivates you and prove to yourself that this motivation is honest and worthwhile. If too many different things motivate you, you'll become tangled up in a maze of all kinds of conflicts. It is imperative to stay focused. Figure out what your motivations are going to be in the next step.

Keep dreaming, but don't daydream: if you do it for praise, you are likely to short-change yourself in the end. Look at success firsthand so that you know how it works and what it costs to achieve it."

However, we must be careful not to let praise make us complacent or worse. Some people let praise go to their heads and are so overly impressed with themselves that they feel they've already made it and stop pushing ahead.

The opposite is also true. When we are criticized or our ideas are rejected, we give up too easily. Sure, we will not always be right, but if we are convinced we are on the right track, we must keep trying to accomplish our goals.

Don't let other people's opinion about you or your dream influence your self-motivation. If they are negative, don't let them discourage you; if they are flattering, don't become complacent.

Inside ourselves, we have to have a clear understanding of where we want to go and confidence in our ability to get there.

Don't fuss about trifles. Don't permit little things—the mere termites of life—to ruin your happiness.

Dale Carnegie

Listen—Challenge—Assess

We should challenge the praise as well as the criticism. Of course, we have to listen to what our boss says about us, but it's also helpful to know what co-workers and subordinates say about us. Equally important is to listen to what our spouse, our father or our mother or our biggest customer or contributor may say about us.

Successful people balance what they hear about themselves from others. We're all human. The boss may pat us on the back because we really deserve it. Then again, the boss may be patting us on the back because he is about to give us an arduous assignment.

It isn't wise or even necessary to look for a sniper behind every tree. Successful people are not cynics. We can't go marching around the world like a hard-core skeptic saying: "Just give me the facts, ma'am."

Not every compliment is phony; not every criticism is a trumped-up charge. That's why we need our own sense of direction and confidence about where we're headed.

We must stay attuned to the truth that there are millions of yardsticks to measure life. Picking the right one at the right time could be one of the biggest clues to self-motivation that can ever be learned. Keep motivated until the goal is reached.

Enjoy Your Work

We spend most of our lives at work. It's certainly easier to sustain a high level of commitment if we enjoy our work. So, we should do everything we can to enjoy ourselves at work. Just remember while we are having fun—it is a place to work! The fun part should support the work part, not detract from it.

Intel's founder and long-time CEO, Andrew Grove strongly believes that self-motivation comes from the satisfaction we get from our accomplishments. Each triumph generates the confidence to seek greater triumphs; each accomplishment leads to more accomplishments. Let's listen to what he has to say about self-motivation:

He lists six pointers that have helped him maintain his self-motivation:

1. *Celebrate achievements*: Try to provide as many interim milestones as you can, and supplant the long-term drive toward reaching a major result with a series of shorter steps. Then, use the occasions when one of these is achieved as an event to celebrate in some small way. However, you shouldn't let any celebration become a distraction to others who work. Poke gentle fun at each other, including the boss. Keep internal competition light.
2. *Rotate jobs*: Even if you stay with one organization, make every effort to rotate jobs occasionally. Even in the best organizations, any job can become tedious after a while. It is harder to create and sustain energy and drive if you have the same job forever. Rotating jobs and working in different assignments is an excellent way to keep your work interesting and to enrich our skills.
3. *Enjoy the people you work with:* Our co-workers are usually very important to us. Our activities at work are almost always connected with theirs. To do our work well, we are dependent on them, and they on us. The people we work with are a major factor in determining whether or not our work is pleasant, congenial, and maybe even fun. Often, our feelings toward the people we work with determine if we like going to work each morning. Problems with co-workers can significantly affect our work and the work of our entire group. Sorting out such problems is important for the benefit of our productivity, as well as for our emotional well-being.

4. *Enjoy the work*: It is impossible to like all of it. Sometimes you will chafe under its unrelenting nature, other times you will be bored, but overall you must enjoy it. Try to see how what you do makes a difference, and approach the work with a bit of zest, maybe even playfulness. Doing so induces a bit of levity when it's most needed and leads to camaraderie.
5. *Be dedicated to the work:* Be dedicated to the end result, the output, not how to get to it or whose idea it is or whether you look good or not. Respect the work of those who respect their work. Nobody is unimportant; it takes many people to make an organization function.
6. *Be straight with everyone:* This isn't an easy principle to stick to. There are various reasons or excuses to compromise a little here or there. We may reason that people are not ready to hear the truth or the bad news, that the time isn't right, or whatever. Giving in to those tempting rationalizations usually leads to conduct that can be ethically wrong and will backfire every time. When stumped, stop and think the way through to meaningful answers.

Believe in what you are doing and in yourself, and want to get something accomplished.

Dale Carnegie

Enrich Your Jobs

Behavioral scientists generally agree that although we are motivated by such external factors as recognition, appreciation, challenge and, of course, fair treatment, the most effective motivator of all is the work itself. If we find our jobs boring and unchallenging, no matter how good these external motivators may be, we will have a tough time motivating ourselves. On the other hand, if we enjoy our work so much that we can't wait to come in every morning and hate to leave each evening, there is little else we need do to keep ourselves motivated.

Unfortunately, a great percentage of jobs in industry today are merely routine, and it is difficult if not impossible, to generate excitement about them. One way to overcome this is to find a way to enrich the job.

Competing Against Ourselves

Denise, a computer operator, works at her home, entering data provided by her employer into computer programs, developing spreadsheets and related assignments.

Once she mastered the techniques, she was able to perform them accurately and meet deadlines readily. After doing this for several months, it became so routine that Denise was easily bored and instead of looking forward to her assignments, she dreaded them and would find excuses to postpone starting her workday.

When her boss rejected her request for more varied work, she tried to find some way to overcome her apathy: "I'm a competitor," she told herself, "if I were in a contest to finish my work faster than my rivals, I would be excited about it. But as I have no rivals, I have to compete against myself."

When she received her next assignment, she timed each phase of it, checked it and corrected errors, and recorded it.

She continued this until she established a norm that factored in variations in the assignments and then competed against this norm on each assignment. The challenge of this competition re-motivated her and she's now thinking of other challenges to build into the job to reinforce her self-motivation.

We Can't Always Do It Alone

When Jennifer was hired as a claims processing clerk at the Liability Insurance Company, she found her job boring and stifling. The claims processing operation was an "assembly line." Each clerk checked a section of the claims form, passed it to the next clerk, who checked the next section, and so on. If an error or question on interpretation was discovered, it was put aside for handling by a specialist. From an operational viewpoint, this was highly efficient. However, it made the work dull and unchallenging. Jennifer spoke to her supervisor about it and suggested that the job would not only be more interesting but more efficient if it could be enlarged. Her supervisor agreed and together they devised a new system. The "assembly line" was replaced by a system in which each clerk checked the entire form, corrected errors and sought interpretations. This required added training and did slow the work down in the beginning, but it paid off not only for Jennifer, but also for the entire department by developing a highly motivated team of workers who were really interested in their jobs. Turnover, absenteeism, and dissatisfaction were significantly reduced, and once the system was fully established, speed and accuracy were increased.

Never Let Discouragement Dominate

One of the most successful men in American industrial history was Charles M. Schwab. Ever since he was a poor boy starting in life he gave himself success treatments.

He never let the determination to be successful and prosperous fade from his mind.If he had allowed himself to yield to the many discouragements he faced, he would never have become a great industrialist. He always triumphed over these negative, destructive, discouraging thoughts, by insisting on holding to the ideal of prosperity and success.

Your ideas, your visions, your resolutions come to you fresh every day. Act now. Another inspiration, new ideas may come tomorrow, but today you should carry out the inspiration of the day.

A vision flashes across the artist's mind with lightning-like rapidity. She keeps turning it over and over in her mind. It takes possession of her very soul, but she is not in her studio, or it is not convenient to put her vision upon canvas, and the picture gradually fades from her mind.

A strong, vigorous conception flashes into the brain of the writer, and he has an almost irresistible impulse to seize his pen and transfer the beautiful images and the fascinating conception to paper; but it is not convenient at the moment, and, while it seems almost impossible to wait, he postpones the writing. The images and the conception keep haunting him, but he still postpones. Finally, the visions grow dimmer and dimmer, and at last fade away and are lost forever.

It is the execution of a plan that creates success. Almost

anybody can resolve to do a great thing; it is only the strong determined character that puts the resolve into execution.

Of course, there are times when the idea or impulse comes at a time when it is not possible to execute it. We are on a long plane flight; we are in the midst of another major project; the idea comes to us in the middle of the night.

Great ideas need not die. Benjamin Franklin always had a pad and pencil handy—in his pocket, at his bedside, on his desk—in which he jotted down ideas as they came to him. He made a point to review these the moment he had time and to take action as soon as he could. Today we can speak or type our ideas into our PDA's or Blackberry's no matter where we may be.

Success Comes From Within

No human being has ever succeeded in trying to be somebody else, even if that person was a success. Success cannot be copied; it cannot be successfully imitated. It is an original force—an individual creation.

If we try to be somebody else and to express somebody else instead of ourselves, we are likely to fail. Power comes from within or from nowhere. We must be ourselves. We must listen to the voice within. There is room for improvement in every profession, in every trade, and in every business. The world wants people who can do things in new and better ways. Don't think, because a plan or idea has no precedent, or because you are young and inexperienced, that you will not get a hearing. If you have anything new and valuable to give to the world, it will be heard and considered. If you dare to think your own thoughts and originate your own methods, if you are not afraid to be yourself, and are not a copy of someone else, you will be recognized. Nothing else will attract the attention of an employer or the rest of the world as quickly as originality and unique ways of doing things, especially if they are effective.

Control Your Thoughts

Considering that mind governs everything in our world, we must channel it to be self-motivated. In recent years, the control of thought, and its use to modify character, to change even external surroundings, or at least their effect on one's self, and to bring about health, happiness, and success, have been more and more studied and understood.

When a task to be done consists largely or wholly of mental acts—as do most ways to gain success—how much greater must be the determining power of the thought. The conquerors of the world, whether on battlefields, in trade or in moral struggles, have won by the attitude of mind in which they motivated themselves to do the work they had to do.

Once we realize the inherent capacity for great things, convinced that we are intended to succeed, and that we can control our minds, we can revolutionize our lives and abolish most of our ills and troubles.

> *You can't get anywhere in this world without wanting to do something.*
>
> *Dale Carnegie*

We cannot expect ourselves to become well and strong by always thinking and talking about our bad health, or assuming that we will never be robust. Neither can we expect our executive faculties to be strong and vigorous if we perpetually doubt our ability to do what we undertake. Nothing so weakens the mind and renders it totally unfit for effective thinking as the constant acknowledgment of weakness, or doubting of our ability to accomplish our goals.

There can be no more important study, no higher duty owed to ourselves, than the understanding of thought-control and of self-motivation, which results in self-development. Perhaps because thought in itself is intangible, and most of us really have so little control over it, there is an impression that directing our minds is a difficult and mysterious affair, something that requires hard study, leisure, and book knowledge to accomplish. Nothing is further from the truth. Whatever the level of our education, the level of our culture, or however busy we may be, all of us have within ourselves all that is required and all the time needed to remake our intellectual nature, our character, and our life.

Every person will have a different task, different problems to solve, and different results to aim at, but the process is practically the same, and the transformation is no more impossible for one than for another.

Let us concentrate on our goal—see it in our minds as though it were already won, while we are all the while intensely conscious of moving nearer to its achievement. One by one obstacles will vanish, and what seemed once too hard for human strength to accomplish appears now plain and even simple. The greatest need of all is to keep the goal in sight and not let interest flag or inward vision waver from the very place in which we most desire to be engaged, in the very work we would love best to accomplish.

There is No Substitute For Work

Thinking about success is not enough. Outward work must follow inward contemplation. True meditation does not absolve us from the need of making effort, but it is a means for revealing to us what efforts we need to make and how to make them. Hold the thought and get to work. Start by holding the right thought, that is, the right mental attitude toward your goals, and then hustle for all you are worth to make your dream come true.

As a matter of fact, nothing happens until the mind moves it. Nothing starts in this world until thought precedes the action. Thought moves everything that is. It is the prime mover of the things we perceive through the senses.

It is the constant thinking about our business, the planning of ways and means to extend it, the schemes for its improvement and betterment that really enlarge it. Our thoughts, our planning, our enthusiasm, our dreaming of success—all these are vital forces that increases the power of our mental magnet to attract the thing we long for.

No matter what the nature of our work or our business, the habit of holding in mind the prosperous ideal, the happiness ideal, the good luck ideal, sets the mind in the direction of these ideals and helps wonderfully in our efforts to always face the light under all circumstances. This mental attitude builds up our confidence in ourselves. When we think more of ourselves, we will be self-motivated and see greater possibilities ahead.

Commitment

One of the most effective ways to motivate ourselves is to be firmly committed to what we desire to accomplish. When things go wrong, when obstacles seem unconquerable, when discouragement raises its face, our commitment will motivate us to keep up the fight.

Champions never say: "It can't be done." They try to find a way to overcome the obstacles. Even champions don't always win, but they never lose without first trying to win because they are committed to win.

Thinking

The basic component of self-motivation is thinking. Before commencing the project, it is essential that it be thought out. A superb performer thinks out how the job will be performed before its beginning.

In a complex operation, as much time must often be given to the planning as to the work itself. Before making a sales call, the successful sales representative thinks carefully about all of the possible problems that may develop and how they can be handled. Executives think about every ramification any of their decisions may cause before making that decision. This is also true of top performers in the theater, cinema, television or in sports. Norman Strauss, an industrial painting contractor in New York City, was faced with a major problem. His bid for the job of painting Madison Square Garden, New York's largest indoor sports arena was due by the end of the week.

The major problem was painting the ceiling, which was 110 feet above the first floor. The usual way of reaching the ceiling was constructing a pipe platform on which the painters would stand when they sprayed the ceiling. The cost of building the platform would be the same for all bidders. The only way to significantly reduce the bid would be to find some way to paint the ceiling without building the pipe platform. Everybody knew this couldn't be done, so why bother?

But Norman Strauss did not give up easily. He was committed to achieve success and ceaselessly devoted himself to solve the problem. On the way home that evening, Norman noticed an electric company repainting a high street light. To reach this light, they were using a "cherry picker," a truck with an elevator on its roof that could be raised to various heights. "Why not use cherry pickers to reach the ceiling at the Garden," Norman thought. The next day investigation brought out that it was feasible and economical. Strauss was able to submit a significantly lower bid than his competitors and obtained the job.

Self-Motivation Must Be Ongoing

Everyone who wants to keep growing, increase his ability, and multiply his talent, must strive to outdo his past records. They must be ready to take advantage of every legitimate opportunity, for personal improvement, for advancement in their business or profession.

Whatever anyone's business is, there is only one way to insure progress and that is by constantly endeavoring to better one's previous records. Spasmodic effort, no matter how vigorous, won't do it. It is the daily progress that counts most in the final averaging.

That we did a fine piece of work, a superb thing yesterday is no reason why we should rest on our laurels today. It should rather spur us to go ahead of it tomorrow.

We must never allow ourselves or anyone else to shake our confidence in ourselves, or to destroy our self-reliance, for this is the very foundation of all great achievement. When that is gone, our whole structure falls; as long as we have it, there is hope for us. Confidence unbounded, unshaken faith in ourselves, which even amounts to boldness at times, is absolutely necessary in all great undertakings.

Sum and Substance

- Follow the lead of successful people—think success-thoughts.
- The best motivator is within our own minds. If we believe in ourselves and in our inevitable success, we create within ourselves a never-ending self-motivating mechanism.
- Don't let other people's opinions about you or your dream influence your self-motivation. If they are negative, don't let it discourage you; if they are flattering, don't become complacent.
- If you enjoy your work so much that you can't wait to come in every morning and hate to leave each evening, there is little else that you need to do to keep yourself motivated.
- If you dare to think your own thought and originate your own methods, if you are not afraid to be yourself, and are not a copy of someone else, you will be quickly recognized.

- All of us have within ourselves all the time and capacity needed to remake our intellectual nature, our character, and our lives.
- Be firmly committed to what you desire to accomplish. When things go wrong, when obstacles seem unconquerable; when discouragement raises its face, your commitment will motivate you to keep up the fight.

6

ACCENTUATE THE POSITIVE

Maintaining a positive attitude is important in every area of the image we project, but nowhere is it more critical than in our attitude toward ourselves. Eleanor Roosevelt is often quoted as saying: "No one can make you feel inferior without your permission."

Most of us—even the most seemingly successful—carry around a mental suitcase full of negative messages about ourselves. Sometimes we do get positive pictures of ourselves from others. As suggested in Chapter 1—hold on to them! Start a file folder or notebook to collect acknowledgment, thank-you notes, stellar reviews, good evaluations, and other tangible evidence of your abilities.

Maintain a Hopeful Attitude

There is nothing else so helpful as the carrying of an optimistic, expectant attitude—the attitude that always looks for and expects the best, the highest, the happiest—and never allowing oneself to get into a pessimistic, discouraged mood.

We must believe with all our heart that we will do what we were made to do. Never for an instant harbor a doubt of it. We must entertain only "thought-friends"—ideals of the thing we are determined to achieve. We must reject all "thought-enemies"—all discouraging moods, everything which would even suggest failure or unhappiness.

It does not matter what we are trying to do or who we are trying to be, so long as we always assume an expectant, hopeful, optimistic attitude regarding it. This will put us on the road to grow all our faculties, and improve.

> *It isn't what you have, or who you are, or where you are, or what you are doing that makes you happy or unhappy. It is what you think about.*
>
> *Dale Carnegie*

Great Achievers Are Positive Thinkers

That one quality of persistently holding the faith in themselves, and never allowing anything to weaken their belief, has been the underlying principle of all great achievers. The great majority of men and women who have given civilization a great uplift started poor, and for many dark years saw no hope of accomplishing their ambition, but they kept on working and believing that somehow a way would be opened. Think of what this attitude of hopefulness and faith has done for the world's great inventors! How most of them plodded on through many years of dry, dreary drudgery before the light came. And the light probably would have never come but for their faith, hope, and persistent endeavor.

There is no other habit which brings so much value to our lives than always expecting the best ought to happen to us, and that of taking for granted that we ought to succeed in whatever task we undertake.

Many people foil their chances of success at the very outset by expecting that they are going to fail—thinking that the chances are against them. In other words, their mental attitude is not favorable to success, which they are after. It sometimes even attracts failure. Success is achieved mentally first. If the mental attitude is one of doubt, the results will correspond. There must be persistent faith and continuous confidence, in order to win.

A wavering, doubting mind brings wavering, doubting results.

Strive for the Rewards of Success

Many people are motivated by tangible rewards. They strongly desire to own a beautiful home, drive a luxury car, dine in expensive restaurants, stay at posh resorts—just be rich.

J. P. Morgan was one of the richest men of his generation. When asked why he continued to be motivated by money when he already had every luxury money can buy, he responded: "Money is the scorecard by which I measure my success. I don't need the money for its own sake, but by continuing to work to increase my wealth, I am proving to myself that I continue to be an achiever."

When Teddy L., one of the top ten sales representatives for his company was asked what motivated him to get out day after day and make call after call, he responded that he came from a poor family, lived in a cold-water flat in a tenement house all of his childhood. "I always dreamed," he said, "that one day I would own a house, a home like those the rich people in my town lived in. When I started selling, I was a mediocre salesman. I made just enough sales to meet my quotas and make a fair income to afford a comfortable apartment. Then one day I drove through the part of town where the rich people lived. I recalled my dream of having a house like theirs. I resolved then and there to make enough money to buy such a home."

"That day I went to a real estate office and obtained photographs of some of the houses in that neighborhood that were for sale. I tacked one of them on the table next to my bed; pasted another on my bathroom mirror; clipped another on the visor in my car. Every night before I went to bed, I looked at the picture; every morning when I shaved, I looked at the picture; every day as I drove to see my customers, I looked at the picture. I resolved that one day I would buy a house like the ones in those photos."

"I could visualize myself and my family living in that house. I could see us dining in the large dining room; relaxing in the parlor; each of my children playing in his own room; my wife cooking in a modern kitchen; all of us enjoying the tree-shaded lawn. These thoughts motivated me to press harder at each sales call; to make one more call each day; to learn and apply more effective sales approaches."

"Over the next few months my sales increased. Within a year my income had doubled and a year later, I was able to buy my dream house."

Rewards do not have to be tangible. Some people seek rewards in the satisfaction of accomplishing their dreams. John Burroughs was a successful man, but he was not a rich man. He lived in modest circumstances. Money was not important to him. He was probably the greatest naturalist of his time. He devoted his life to studying and writing about nature.

He received his reward from the great satisfaction of being among the wonders of nature. He said: "I live to broaden and enjoy my own life, believing that in doing so, I am doing what is best for everyone. If I ran after birds only to write about them, I should never have written anything that anyone else would have cared to read. I must write from sympathy and love—that is for enjoyment—or not at all. The work is pleasure and hence, the result gives pleasure."

By keeping in the front of our minds the reward we seek whether it is tangible—a new car, a fine home, money for our retirement, or intangible—satisfaction of accomplishing our dream, we will be motivated to work hard to achieve that goal and reap that reward.

Don't Look For Trouble

Some people always look at the dark side of every situation. Considering how unprofitable such efforts are, it is surprising how many people make a business of looking for trouble, or cultivating and coaxing it. No one ever looked for trouble yet found plenty of it. This is because one can make trouble out of anything if the mind is set that way. It is said that during the development of the West, in the days of rough frontier life, the men who always went armed with pistols, revolvers, and bowie-knives always got into difficulties, while the men who never carried arms, but trusted their own good sense, self-control, tact and humor, rarely got into trouble. The incident that meant a shooting affray to the armed men was merely a joke to the more sensible unarmed men. It is just so with the seekers of ordinary trouble. By constantly holding discouraged, dejected, melancholy, gloomy thoughts, they make themselves receptive to all that depresses and destroys. What to a cheerful person would be a trifling incident, to be laughed at and dismissed from the mind, becomes in the mind of the croaker, a thing of dread, an occasion for gloom and foreboding.

Imagination wrongly used, is one of our worst foes. There are people who live in perpetual unhappiness and discomfort because they imagine they are being abused, slighted, neglected, and talked about. They think of themselves as a target of all sorts of evils, being the object of envy, jealously, and all kinds of ill will. Most such ideas are delusions and have no reality whatsoever. This is the most unfortunate state of mind to get into. It kills happiness, it demoralizes usefulness, it throws the mind out of harmony, and life itself becomes unsatisfactory.

People who think such thoughts make themselves perpetually wretched by surrounding themselves with an atmosphere reeking with pessimism. It is as if they are always wearing dark glasses, which makes everything around them seem draped in mourning; they see nothing but black. There is nothing cheerful or bright in their world.

These people have talked poverty, failure, hard luck, fate, and hard times so long that their entire being is imbued with pessimism.

The cheerful qualities of the mind have atrophied from neglect and disuse, while their pessimistic tendencies have been so overdeveloped that their minds cannot regain a normal, healthy, cheerful balance.

These people carry a gloomy, disagreeable, uncomfortable influence with them wherever they go. Nobody likes to converse with them, because they are always telling their stories of hard luck and misfortune. With them, times are always hard, money scarce, and society "going to the bad." After a while they become pessimistic cranks with morbid minds, and people avoid them.

The most injurious and unpleasant way of looking for trouble is faultfinding, or continual criticism of other persons. Some people are never generous, never magnanimous toward others. They are stingy of their praise, rarely recognize merit in others, and are critical of their every act.

> *If you believe in what you are doing, then let nothing hold you up in your work. Much of the best work of the world has been done against seeming impossibilities.*
>
> *Dale Carnegie*

Don't Criticize, Condemn or Complain

We should make up our minds firmly at the very outset in life that we will not criticize or condemn others, or find fault with their mistakes and shortcomings. Faultfinding, indulging in sarcasm and irony, picking flaws in everything and everybody, looking for things to condemn instead of praise is a very dangerous habit to possess. It is like a deadly worm that gnaws at the heart of the rosebud or fruit, and will make life gnarled, distorted, and bitter.

No life can be harmonious and happy after this blighting habit is once formed. Those who always look for something to condemn ruin their own character and destroy their normal integrity.

We all like sunshiny, bright, cheerful, hopeful people; nobody likes the grumbler, the faultfinder, the backbiter or the slanderer. The great American philosopher, Ralph Waldo Emerson wrote: "the world likes the man who sees longevity in his causes and good in the future, who believes the best and not the worst of people."

Idle gossipers, serpent tongues, people who give vent to their tempers get only momentary satisfaction, and even afterward they are tormented by their own ugly natures and then wonder why people enjoy their lives and they do not enjoy theirs.

It is just as easy to go through life looking for the good and the beautiful, instead of the ugly; for the noble instead of the ignoble; for the bright and cheerful instead of the dark and gloomy; the hopeful instead of the despairing; to see the bright side instead of the dark side. To set our face always toward the sunlight is just as easy as to always see the shadows, and it makes all the difference in our character between content and discontent, between happiness and misery, between prosperity and adversity, between success and failure.

Let us learn to look for the light, positively refuse to harbor shadows and blot, negative images. Let us hold to those things that give pleasure, that are helpful and inspiring, in order to change our whole way of looking at things, and transform our personality in a very short time.

Optimism Leads to Achievement

Helen Keller, the blind and deaf woman who had every reason to bemoan her fate and be pessimistic said: "Optimism is the faith that leads to achievement, nothing can be done without hope."

The people who have succeeded in life have always been cheerful and hopeful people, who went about their business with a smile on their faces, and took the changes and chances of this mortal life as mature adults, facing rough and smooth phases of life alike.

Optimistic people have a creative power that pessimistic people never possess. There is nothing which will so completely sweeten life and take out its drudgery, nothing that will so effectively ease the jolts on the road, as a sunny, hopeful, optimistic disposition. With the same mental ability, the optimistic thinker has infinitely more power than the despondent, gloomy pessimist. Optimism is a perpetual lubricator of the mind; it is the oil of gladness that drives out friction, worries, anxieties, and disagreeable experiences. The life machinery of an optimist does not wear out as rapidly as people whose moods and temper scour, throwing the entire machinery out of harmony.

Change Negativism Into Positivism

Negativism never accomplish anything. There is no life in a negative person; nothing but deterioration, destruction, and death. Negativism is a great enemy of those who seek success. People who are always talking down to everyone, who are always complaining of hard times and bad business, poor health and poverty, attract all the destructive, negative influences about them, and neutralize all of their endeavors.

The creative principles cannot live in a negative, destructive atmosphere, and no single achievement can take place there. Therefore, negative people are always on the downgrade, always turning out failures. They lose the power of affirmation, and drift, unable to get ahead.

Negativism will paralyze ambition; poison our life; rob us of power. They will kill our self-confidence until we become victims of the situation instead of masters of it. The power to do is largely a question of self-faith and self-confidence. No matter what we undertake, we can never do it until we think we can. We will never master it until we first feel the mastery and do the deed in our minds. It must be thought out or it can never be wrought out. It must be a mentally accomplished before it can be a materially accomplished.

Many people scatter thoughts of fear, doubt, and failure, wherever they go; these take root in minds that might otherwise be free from them and therefore happy, confident, and successful.

Be sure that when you hold an evil or discordant thought toward another, something is wrong in your mind. You should call: "Halt! About face!" Look toward the sunlight; determine that if you cannot do any good in the world, you will not scatter seeds of poison and hatred.

If you hold kindly, charitable, magnanimous, loving thoughts toward everybody, you will not depress or hinder them, but will scatter sunshine and gladness instead of sadness and shadow; project help and encouragement instead of discouragement.

There are people who are always radiating thoughts of success, good health, joy, scattering sunshine wherever they go. These are the helpers of the world, the lighteners of burdens, and the people who ease the jolts of life and soothe the wounded and give solace to the discouraged.

You can be like them by learning to radiate joy, not stingy, or meanly, but generously. You must learn to emit gladness without reserve, to express it in the home, on the street, in the car, in the store, everywhere.

The best way to keep out darkness is to keep the life filled with light; to keep out negative thoughts, keep it filled with harmony; to shut out error, keep the mind filled with truth; to shut out ugliness, contemplate beauty and loveliness; to get rid of all that is sour and unwholesome, and contemplate all that is sweet and wholesome. Opposite thoughts cannot occupy the mind at the same time.

We should form the habit of erasing from the mind all disagreeable, unhealthy, death-dealing thoughts. We should start out every morning with a clean slate, blotting out from our mental gallery all discordant pictures, replacing them with the harmonious, uplifting, life-giving ones.

When Frank A., a successful Chicago marketing executive, was asked by a television interviewer how he "kept his cool" under the day to day pressures of his job, he responded that he never allowed himself to go to his office in the morning until he has put his mind into perfect harmony with the world.

If he had the slightest feeling of envy or jealousy, if he felt selfish or unfair, without the right attitude toward his partner or any of his employees, he simply did not go to work until his instrument was in tune, until his mind was clear of any form of discord. He said he discovered that if he starts out in the morning with a right attitude of mind toward everybody, he would infinitely get more out of his day than otherwise; that whenever he allowed himself to go to work in the past with negative thoughts dominating his mind, he did not obtain nearly as good results and he made those about him unhappy, to say nothing of the increased wear and tear upon himself.

Substitute Harmony For Discord

No matter whether we feel positive or not, we must affirm that we *do* feel positive, that we *will* feel positive, and that we are in a position to do our best to act positively. Say it deliberately, affirm it vigorously, and it will come true.

As the Bible says: "As a man thinketh in his heart, so is he." Many people who do only mediocre things really have a great deal of ability, but are so sensitive to friction that they cannot do effective work. If they only had someone to steer them, to plan for them, to keep discord away from them and help them to create harmony, they could do remarkable things. As most of us do not have such a "guardian angel," we must acquire this for ourselves. No one can exercise it for us, and we cannot accomplish anything very great in this world unless we are able to avoid succumbing to the thousand and one things that distract us. Unfortunately, there are times when we are disagreeable and irritable. This is not our real nature. The cause of our irritability and lack of harmony is because we are tired or stressed. We must learn to recognize when this may happen and make every effort to overcome it.

We often see people who have become absolutely unbearable, after a year of hard work, completely revolutionized when they return from a holiday or a vacation. They do not seem like the same people that they were before they went away. The trifles that would throw them into a fit of passion before their vacation do not affect them at all now.

As a squeaking axle indicates the want of a lubricant, friction or discord anywhere in the physical economy is a warning that something is wrong. A dispute at the breakfast table, or any little wrangling in the morning may destroy the peace of the household for the entire day. A moment's hot temper may destroy a very dear friendship for life.

In pursuing our daily activities, we force ourselves to work when we are tired and out of tune; when our spontaneity is gone, and our vital standards are low. We force ourselves by all sorts of stimulants and will power. We strain the delicate mechanism or our minds and bodies until they are often prematurely injured, overstrained, ruined for their finest work.

We ought to school ourselves in a way that no matter what happens we would not lose our presence of mind, and balance. We should always keep our equilibrium so as to be able, no matter what happens, to do the levelheaded thing, the wise thing, the right thing.

> *Remember happiness doesn't depend upon who you are or what you have; it depends solely on what you think.*
>
> *Dale Carnegie*

Self-Defeating Thought Patterns

Many times we find ourselves doubting our abilities and our accomplishments due to our lack of self-confidence and negative surroundings. To make matters worse, we emphasize and dwell on what others think in order to determine how we feel about our ability and ourselves. This mindset can lead us to avoid taking risks due to fear of failure. This kind of reinforcement can lead us to put ourselves down, discount positive feedback and subscribe to harmful assumptions that perpetuate self-defeating thought patterns and a negative attitude. Some self-defeating thought patterns include:

Extreme thinking

When things become all or nothing and there is no middle ground. We tend to think: "I am a total failure when my performance is not perfect."

Imminent disaster

Disaster lurks around in every corner and comes to be expected. For example, a single negative detail, piece of criticism, or passing comment darkens all reality. Our concern: "I blew the small presentation and now I'll never get promoted."

Magnification of the negative

Good things don't count nearly as much as bad ones. This leads us to feel: "I know I had the best sales record the last three months, but coming in third this month makes me feel terrible about myself."

Overemphasis on "should" statements

"Should" statements are meant to push us toward the perfect scenario. In order to achieve what should be, we must first assess the *as is* situation. Once this is established, we can plan on how to get from where we are now to the "should be." Just because we are not as yet close to the "should be" we should not be detered from moving forward and working toward it.

Boxing in

Boxing ourselves is a non-rational thought process in which we blame ourselves. It is easy to let initial defeats determine our long-term mindset. Don't fall into the trap of thinking: "I am a failure and I'll never be anything else."

Difficulty accepting compliments

When receiving a compliment, we should accept it and not mitigate it with comments like: "You like this presentation? It was nothing. I have done better." Say: "Thank you." In this way you indicate to the compliment giver that you appreciate his or her comments, but more importantly, you reinforce your own self-confidence and self-image.

Strategies for Developing Confidence

These self-defeating thoughts can turn us from optimists to pessimists, from positive to negative thinkers, from success oriented to defeat doomed. The following strategies may help us overcome self-defeating thought patterns:

Self-acceptance

Self-acceptance comes from our ability to accept ourselves as human beings while focusing on our positive sides—our qualities, strengths, and traits—that make us who we are. When our focus is upon these areas of our self-image both confidence and self-esteem are positively influenced. It is all too common for people to focus upon their weaknesses instead of their strengths and therefore do more damage than good. We must help ourselves, and others to focus on the positive pictures.

Self-respect

The key here is to focus on our past success and achievements and to respect ourselves for the good we have done in the past. It is far easier to dwell on failures since others are only too eager to point them out to us. When we spend our time contemplating the many successes we all have in our lives, our perspective changes, followed by our confidence.

Thought Control

There can be no better study, no higher duty owed to ourselves than that of thought-control, which results in self-development. Perhaps because thought in itself is intangible, and most of us really have so little control over it, there is an impression that direction of mind's action is a difficult and complex affair, something that requires hard study, leisure, and book knowledge to accomplish. Nothing is further from the truth. We have within ourselves all that is required, and all the time needed, to remake our intellectual nature, our character, and practically our entire life.

Concentrate on the goal

We must concentrate on our committed goal, to see before the mental eye the prize as though it were already won. Then, one by one obstacles will vanish, and what once seemed too hard for us to accomplish would now appear plain and even simple. The greatest need of all is to keep the goal in sight and not let interest flag or inward vision waver.

Sum and Substance

- There is no better uplifting habit than that of bearing a hopeful attitude, of believing that things are going to turn out well and not ill; that we are going to succeed and not fail; that no matter what may or may not happen, we are going to be happy.
- Whatever comes to us in life we create first in our minds. As the building is a reality in all its details in the architect's mind before a stone or brick is laid, so we create everything mentally that later becomes a reality with our achievement.
- By mental visualization of the ideal as vividly and sharply as possible will make our dream come true. By imagining something we truly want with the whole mind, and heart, and soul, by imagining it as if it were already true, will move it to its fruition.
- We need to tell our subconscious exactly what we want. When we know what our true desire really is, our subconscious mind will propel us unerringly towards it. We must believe

that what we want can happen. We must believe that it will happen.

- All great achievers have had the quality of holding the persistently faith in themselves, and never allowing anything to weaken the belief that somehow they will accomplish what they undertook.
- Success is achieved mentally first. If the mental attitude is one of doubt, the results will correspond. There must be persistent faith and continuous confidence in order to win. A wavering, doubting mind brings wavering, doubting results.
- There is no other habit which would bring as much value to our lives as that of always expecting the best of taking it for granted that we are going to win in whatever we undertake.
- The reason why so many people fail to realize their ideals is that they are not willing to do their part to make it real. The longing, the desire to do a certain thing, is merely sowing the seed of our ambition. We must back up that which our heart longs to realize with an honest purpose to do our best and an earnest effort to make our vision real.
- Power comes from within or from nowhere. Listen to the voice within. There is room for improvement in every profession, in every trade, and in every business. The world wants people who can do things in new and better ways. Because our plan or idea has no precedent, or because we are young and inexperienced, we fear that we will not get a hearing. If we have anything new and valuable to give to the world, we will be heard and followed.
- Until we erase "fate" and "can't" and "doubt" from our vocabulary, we cannot rise. We cannot get strong while we

harbor convictions of our weakness or be happy while we dwell on our miseries or misfortunes.

- Be firmly committed to what you desire to accomplish. When things go wrong, when obstacles seem unconquerable, when discouragement raises its face, our commitment will motivate us to keep up the fight.

7

BE COURAGEOUS

The determination to succeed and the willpower to exert the energy and time, to sacrifice immediate pleasures, to fight opposition, to overcome obstacles and challenges in the pursuit of our goals, is an essential ingredient on the road to success.

Successful people have the courage to put their ideas into effect, the willingness to put their money, their efforts, their emotions into an enterprise in which they truly believe.

While these achievers display astonishing boldness, they are not reckless gamblers. They prepare their moves with a ferocious intensity, and then fly into action.

We must take risks if we want to be better than average people. We cannot always "play it safe." Security is mostly a superstition. It does not exist in nature, nor do people in general experience it. Striving to avoid all danger can end up being no safer in the long run than outright exposure. Life is either a daring adventure, or nothing.

The great US Supreme Court Justice, Oliver Wendell Holmes puts it this way: "Security is an illusion, and repose is not the destiny of man."

Whether it be in the world of business, sports, or politics, the men and women who have achieved great success have manifested their courage by defying the odds, by jumping into dangerous waters, by making creative decisions; they have risked losing all because they never doubted that they would succeed.

The most dangerous situation in the world is that of people who have given up, who do not try to help themselves, who make no efforts to rise. No power in the world can do all the lifting. God Himself will not help those who will not help themselves. The determination to succeed is the ladder of our ascent. We must make sure that there are no weak rungs in our ladder.

We must develop the strength of our resolution. Unless our convictions are on the surface, we stand for nothing. Nobody will have confidence in us. Unless conviction takes hold of one's very being, there will be very little achievement in life.

Approach new experiences as opportunities to learn rather than occasions to win or lose. Doing so opens us up to new possibilities and can increase our sense of self-acceptance. Not doing so turns every possibility into an opportunity for failure, and inhibits personal growth.

> *Take a chance! All life is a chance. The man who goes furthest is generally the one who is willing to do and dare. The "sure thing" boat never gets far from shore.*
>
> *Dale Carnegie*

Become Involved

When Alex was a boy in Chicago, he and his friends were ardent Cubs fans. They were elated when their team won and unhappy when they lost. Alex felt the losses more than his friends. When the Cubs lost, he would be deeply depressed. After a particularly bad season, Alex thought: "It isn't worth it. I'm never going to get so involved with a team that I can feel this bad." From that time on he refused to commit himself to the Cubs or any team in any sport.

Alex carried this concept into all aspects of his life. His philosophy was: "If I don't become too involved, I can never be hurt." In his school and in his jobs, he always took the middle course. Indeed, Alex never did get hurt, but neither did he ever have any real joys. By not taking the chance that someone or something he supported might not work out, he avoided the "agony of defeat," but never experienced "the thrill of victory."

Be Committed

Dr. Robert Jarvik worked for years to develop an artificial heart. It had never been done and he was told by colleagues and other "experts" that it never could be done. Jarvik was not only willing to take the chance that all of his work would be for naught, but he was committed to keep trying until he did succeed.

Inventors and innovators have always faced ridicule. We have read how Fulton's steamboat was dubbed "Fulton's FOLLY" and how the first automobiles were greeted with the scornful accusation—"Get a horse." Edison had tried and failed hundreds of times before succeeding in inventing the light bulb. Inventors must commit themselves and be willing to suffer the taunts of others and bear the many doubts and disappointments of defeat after defeat before reaching their goals.

Don't Fear Dissent

Liz was upset. All of the people in the group seemed to agree that the idea under discussion would solve their problem. If she expressed her disagreement, the others might consider her stupid, or worse, a rebel. The safe course was to remain silent, but Liz was sure that the group had overlooked an important aspect of the problem. Liz took the risk of being rejected, but by saying what she believed, she enabled the group to look at the problem from a different angle and come to a more effective conclusion.

Taking risks does not mean one must be a daredevil. Reasonable people take reasonable risks, but by definition, a risk may not succeed. Successful business executives take risks with every decision they make. However, they maximize their chance of success by careful research and analysis before making the decision. But when that decision finally has to be made, the manager must be willing to risk the possible loss of money, time, energy and emotion. Without risk, there is no possibility of gain.

Prepare to Accept the Worst

In chapter 1, we learned that Dale Carnegie in his book *How to Stop Worrying and Start Living,* advised that when facing trouble: "Ask yourself: What is the worst that can possibly happen?" "Prepare to accept the worst; then try to improve on it."

We should use these principles when we have to make a decision on whether or not to take a chance on an innovative, radical or just different approach to a problem.

We must all take risks if we want to make progress in our jobs and in our lives. By careful analysis we can minimize the chances of failure, but we can never eliminate it. Without pain there is no gain. By always playing it safe, we may avoid that pain, but we will never feel the great joy and satisfaction that results from overcoming the obstacles and reaching our goals.

> *Most of us have far more courage than we ever dreamed we possessed.*
>
> *Dale Carnegie*

Have Faith

We cannot hope to succeed if we are timid, lack faith in ourselves, and do not have the courage of our convictions. We cannot always seek for certainty before we venture. Self-distrust is the cause of most of our failures. In the assurance of strength there is strength, and they are the weakest, who have no faith in themselves or their powers.

The failure, which overtakes so many merchants, is due, not so much to their lack of business talent, as to their lack of business nerve. We see many people who are endowed with brilliant capacities, but are cursed with indecision. They are prone to follow the instincts of a weak nature against the utilization of clear intelligence. The world is overcrowded with people who remain stationary, filling minor positions, and drawing meager salaries, simply because they have never thought it worth while to achieve mastery in the pursuits they have chosen to follow.

There are some people whose failure to succeed in life is a problem to others, as well as to themselves. They are industrious, prudent, and economical; yet after a long life of striving, old age finds them still poor. They complain of ill luck, they say fate is against them, but the real truth is that their projects miscarry because they mistake mere activity for energy. Confounding two things essentially different, they suppose that if they are always busy they must necessarily be advancing their fortunes, forgetting that misdirected labor is a waste of activity.

Courage Converts Dreams to Reality

One reason why many people do not achieve their goals is that they seem to look upon their dream, their ambition as a sort of fanciful mental picture, something that has no definite basis in reality. These people never take their life mission very seriously, and consequently never grow to their full stature.

They do not seem to realize that to make those dreams come true, they were meant to play definite and distinct individual parts in its accomplishment. Yet that is just what we are here to do. We were not thrown off as independent, unrelated units of the universe. People who have faith in themselves feel that their abilities can make their dreams a reality.

Abraham Lincoln was a very modest, unassuming man. When the first rumblings of the Civil War reverberated through the North and a presidential election was at hand, he put himself forward as leader of the nation. When the politicians were looking round for a suitable man for that great position,

Lincoln asked them why they did not nominate him. He said he felt within his breast the power to carry the nation through the threatened crises, and that he believed he would be elected. Coming from a less modest man this assurance would look like a boast, but Lincoln's motives were pure, and his faith, based upon a marvellous dedication for the work to be done, carried him to success.

The history makers have always had strong convictions with regard to their life work. They have believed in their vision, and the part they were to play. They have believed that their ambition foreshadowed a prophecy that it was the substance of things expected, and not a mere figment of the imagination.

In other words, people who have won out in the world have been profound believers in their destiny. The faith of such people impress us with a conviction of their power. We all feel that there is something about people who believe in their destiny that commands our respect, and homage. The world itself makes way for those who believe they were born to play a grand part in the human drama.

Lech Walesa—Liberator of Poland

One of the best examples of courage in recent times is Lech Walesa. Shakespeare said that some people are born great, some achieve greatness and others have greatness thrust upon them. Lech Walesa fits the latter. He seems to have come out of nowhere to lead his people in their fight against

Communist oppression at a time when there was no Polish leader who would stand up to the tyrannical government.

As an electrician at the Lenin Shipyards in Gdansk, he was among the first to express discontent with the Communist government of Poland that was so dominated by the Soviet Union that Poland had become nothing more than a puppet state. As a religious Roman Catholic, he was bitter about the suppression of the church by the Communists.

Walesa was not alone, of course. Most of the workers at the shipyard had been disillusioned by the so-called "workers' paradise" that the Communists had proclaimed. Meanwhile, the unrest at the shipyard was growing stronger. The union members formed what at first was a secret group, which they named "Solidarity"—a word that had traditionally been the watchword of the union movement signifying the solidarity of workers against capitalists. Now this name took on a new meaning—a solid front of workers against the communists. Walesa stood out as leader of this group.

Why did he take on this awesome responsibility, even though knew that this could lead to arrest, imprisonment and perhaps torture by the police or even his death. He knew that he was putting his family in jeopardy?

Years later, when asked if he was afraid, he admitted that he was very much afraid, but he knew that somebody had to take the lead. He remembered the words of the one man he admired most, Pope John Paul II. "Learn to Conquer Fear," the pope had admonished. Walesa heeded the pope's powerful words.

Imprisonment and release

With such a mission in mind, Walesa stepped forward into history. His courageous stand at the Gdansk shipyards thrust him into the public eye all over the world. But it also resulted in a series of persecutions that tested Walesa's courage. He was arrested in 1981 and under martial law was interned in a hunting lodge in a remote part of the country for eleven months.

When he was finally released, a crowd estimated at 1,500 assembled outside his apartment building greeted him. Walesa's emotional and long-awaited homecoming demonstrated that he was still a leader of considerable charisma and, whether the Communist authorities liked it or not, an enormous political force in Poland.

He promised them: "In my future conduct I will be courageous but also prudent, and there is nothing negotiable in this regard. I will talk and act, not on my knees, but with prudence."

Over the next few years, both he and his wife, Danuta, were harassed by the police, brought in for interrogation —sometimes for several days—but he no longer feared them. Because he met with other leaders of Solidarity, he was threatened with another period of detention.

However in the end, the Polish government was reluctant to press the matter much further. After his release, Walesa told journalists that he had been ordered by his interrogators not to meet with Solidarity leaders again but, said the defiant Walesa: "I'll do it again. I will have another meeting."

The Nobel Peace Prize

Walesa was awarded the Nobel Peace prize in 1983. The news of his courage in the face of his defiance of the powerful Communist government drew cheers and praise around the world. Ronald Reagan hailed it as "a triumph of moral force over brute force." John Paul II, whose first return to his homeland in 1979 helped launch the Solidarity movement, sent Walesa a congratulatory telegram in which he applauded the award's "special eloquence." In the official citation, the five members of Norway's Nobel Peace Prize committee praised Walesa's fight for "the workers' right to establish their own organizations," adding that "a campaign for human rights is a campaign for peace."

Lech Walesa's courage was a major contributor to the demise of the Communist government in Poland once the protection from the Soviet Union no longer existed to support it. In 1990, Walesa, the brave electrician from Gdansk was elected president of Poland.

What Walesa's accomplishment teach us:

- No matter how humble our background, if we have courage and the commitment to pursue our goals, nothing can stop us.
- Like Walesa, we may have "greatness thrust upon us." Our challenge is not to fight oppression, but to achieve success. Our opportunity may be starting a business of our own or developing an uncharted sales territory. We may fear the consequences, but if we have confidence in ourselves, we will overcome obstacles and succeed.

Take the High Road

Barry and Leon were among the people laid off when a business in Milwaukee downsized. Leon looked upon this as a great disappointment and misfortune. He showed it in the depressed expression that marked his features. He looked as though he had lost his best friend and his last dollar. His shoulders drooped, his feet dragged, and his clothing was soiled and creased. He complained that he believed he had been born under an unlucky star; that he had been employed by that firm for several years, and had been faithful, loyal and hard working, yet, he had been discharged. He could see no use in trying again, because, he argued, if he had not been able to win out in the work in which he was experienced he did not see how he could be successful in anything else. He felt convinced he was a failure. This thought dominated his thinking and he came to believe that failure was his destiny. It was easy to see that this young man was suffering greatly from that demoralizing disease of discouragement.

On the other hand, Barry took an entirely different view of his layoff. He got up each morning with the attitude that this was a new opportunity for him. He continued to dress as neatly as if he were going to work. There was no sign of defeat in his face. His attitude was that of a winner. There was a look of determination, almost of defiance, in his eye. He appeared so cheerful and happy that friends thought he must have secured a good position. He informed them, however, that he was still hunting for a job; but declared that he had not the slightest doubt he would soon find one, and a better one than he had lost. He said—not boastfully but with an air of quiet conviction—that he would show the company who had discharged him that they did not know what they were giving up; that he had no intention of remaining a perpetual clerk or a perpetual anything else; that he intended to climb to the top; to be an employer himself, and he wanted the firm who had once been his employer to watch his progress.

Barry went on to get into business himself and became a

bigger success than his former employer ever was. Time would undoubtedly show him at the head of a larger business, and would prove that he has greater executive ability, more push, greater initiative, more originality, and resourcefulness than his former company had realized.

Now the difference between these two young employees marks the difference between a winner and a loser. The winner is a person who gets up after he has been knocked down, with more determination than before; a person who is stung into greater activity by some serious setback. A temporary failure does not mean much to such a person—it is only an episode in his life.

> *If you want to develop courage, do the thing you fear to do and keep doing it until you get a record of successful experiences behind you. This is the quickest and surest way ever yet discovered to conquer fear.*
>
> *Dale Carnegie*

Richard Branson—Courage in Business

Richard Branson, the entrepreneur who revolutionized the music industry when he established Virgin Records always sought new challenges. In 1984, he sold his company and decided to engage in an entirely new venture. He started Virgin Atlantic Airways. Why an airline? In the music business Branson traveled constantly and was appalled by the poor service that most airlines provided. Creating an airline that was truly customer conscious was a challenge that appealed to him. Like many entrepreneurs, he drew upon his direct personal experience as a customer in creating a new venture.

His boldness is exemplified by the act that he knew next to nothing about airlines. But, by this time he did know a lot about being an entrepreneur.

To develop an appeal before to the public, he took advantage of being a small company unhindered by bureaucratic red tape. He offered inexpensive flights between Newark Airport near New York City to Gatwick airport near London. Just as he had built Virgin Records by offering discounted prices, he now offered discounted airfares—appealing to the young consumers eager to save cash.

His strategy was simple: Develop an airline that he would like to fly on. Many people have ideas about such products or services, but only a true entrepreneur has the boldness to act on his ideas. Branson was such a man. Many observers thought he did not stand a chance competing against well-heeled British Airways. This did not deter Branson, and he plowed ahead.

It took several years of major losses before Virgin Atlantic began to make money. Despite advice by bankers and friends to give up before he lost all of his money, Branson pushed on. When asked by a newspaper reporter how one can become a multi-millionaire, Branson quipped, "A multi-millionaire is a billionaire who invested in an airline."

Today Virgin Atlantic flies to cities all over the world and is highly profitable. It is now the second largest British long haul international airline and operates a fleet of Boeing 747 and Airbus A340 aircraft to New York, Miami, Boston, Los Angeles, Orlando, San Francisco, Hong Kong, Athens, and Tokyo.

Branson's courage has extended into his personal life.

His participation in record setting boat and balloon races exemplify this courage.

What Branson's story can teach us:

- It isn't necessary to invent or create a new product or service to become a success. Branson studied the market and sought businesses that were already mature, but in his judgment, he sought to provide a better, more efficient or less expensive approach.
- Success involves risk. Branson took risks in all his ventures. Most notably in competing with the well-established British Airways. Branson found a niche that BA had neglected and Virgin Atlantic filled it by offering lower cost and better services.
- Branson had the courage of his convictions. He believed that his ventures would succeed and he didn't give up—even suffering years of losses—until success was his.
- If we contemplate going into a new venture or are currently engaged in our own business, we should keep Branson's experience in mind. If we truly believe in the product or service we are providing, we should have the courage to enter competitive markets. Branson didn't gamble. He was willing to take prudent risks based on the evaluation of a situation. He knew the odds and only took a risk when he felt things were in his favor.

Use It or Lose It

One reason why so many employees never reach the heights is because they cease trying to climb. They have never properly cultivated their ambition, never furnished the fuel that would keep it burning, growing brighter and larger. The decay of ambition in youth, its early deterioration is a sign of early decay in the individual. With the decline of ambition, determination and courage decline.

On the other hand, young people who keep the fires of their ambition burning brightly, who guard their ideal, cannot help turning out well. Those who let it sag, peter out in a short time, never amount to anything. Many a youth who felt confident that they would head up a corporation did nothing to feed their ambition, and today they are nobodies, of little value to themselves or the world.

No matter how conspicuous or well defined our talent, unless we exercise it continuously it will deteriorate. Nature's law, "Use or lose," is operative everywhere. There is no getting away from or ignoring it. Whether it is ambition, talent, or a seed planted in the ground, the law is inevitable. That which is not used, taken care of, or cultivated will slide backward.

Think of Achievement

By setting our minds toward achievement, everything about us would indicates success. We must express this in our manner, our dress, our bearing, and our conversation. Everything we do should speak of achievement and success.

It's a wonderful advantage in starting out every morning with the mind set toward success and achievement, by permeating it with thoughts of prosperity and harmony, whether by repetition of set formulas as some advise, or by concentrating our minds on what we are determined to accomplish. It will then be so much harder for discord to get into the day's work. If we are inclined to doubt our ability to do any particular thing, we must train ourselves to keep the thought that we have the courage to move forward firmly and persistently. It is the assumption of power, of self-trust, of confidence in ourselves, in our integrity, and our courage that cannot be shaken, that will enable us to become strong, and to do, with vigor and ease, the thing we undertake.

We will find that the perpetual holding of these ideals will change our whole outlook upon life. We will approach our problems from a new standpoint, and life will take on a fresh meaning. This perpetual affirmation will put us in harmony with our surroundings; it will make us content and happy. It will help us to build up individuality and personal willpower. It will make our brains clearer, our thoughts more effective. Keeping the mental machinery clean makes for vigorous thinking and decisive action.

Strengthen Courage and Defeat Fears

If we are deficient in any quality, we can strengthen it by constant affirmation. If we lack courage anywhere in our nature (and most people do), we can strengthen courage by constantly affirming that we are absolutely fearless, that we are courageous, that nothing can harm us. Reason that fear is simply the sense of danger, and when we have perfect confidence in ourselves, there will be no cause for fear.

Every time you feel a sense of fear come over you say: "I am absolutely fearless; there is nothing to fear; fear is not a reality; it is not the truth of being. It is only the absence of courage, based upon ignorance of the great cause." Emerson knew the virtue of this philosophy when he said: "Nerve us with incessant affirmation. Don't bark against the bad, but chant the beauties of the good."

Determine not to harbor anything in the mind that you do not wish to become real in your lives. Shun poisoned thoughts, ideas that depress and makes you unhappy as instinctively as you avoid physical danger of any kind. You must replace discordant or unhappy thoughts, or thoughts of weakness and misery with cheerful, hopeful, optimistic thoughts. Form the habit of suggesting to yourself some agreeable or pleasant subject, to dwell upon or think about, or take up some word or idea that will suggest pleasure, happiness, and harmony. You will be surprised to see how quickly you can change the whole course of your thoughts. When your thoughts are changed, your feelings will change. It will increase your courage and confidence, and this is half the battle won.

The Self-Talk

As noted in the first chapter of this book, when our fears or discouragement begin to enter our minds, by giving ourselves a pep talk we can strengthen our resolution. The self-talk is simply a way to create an argument that would hold up to scrutiny due to the weight of the evidence. The stronger and more compelling the evidence is, the more believable and powerful the message. It is an internal discussion we all must have from time to time. This is a tool to take back control of the only thing we should have ultimate control over all the time—our thinking.

> *Inaction breeds doubt and fear. Action breeds confidence and courage. If you want to conquer fear, do not sit home and think about it. Go out and get busy.*
>
> *Dale Carnegie*

Make a Decision and Do It

Chief among the causes that bring total failure or a disappointing result that or only a partial success is vacillation.

Many entrepreneurs have made their fortunes by promptly deciding at some nice juncture to take a considerable risk. Yet many failures are caused by poorly thought out changes and needless vacillation. Determined people, who know what they want to do and do it, always push; vacillators, however strong in other respect, fall behind in the race of life.

If you are vacillators, if you have acquired a habit of hesitating, or of weighting and considering and reconsidering, never quite knowing what you want, you will never be leaders.

This is not the stuff which leaders are made, for whatever else leaders may lack, they know their own minds. They know what they want, and make straight for it. They may make mistakes, they may fall down now and then, but they always get up promptly and push on.

People who decide quickly can afford to make mistakes; for no matter how many they make, they will get on faster than those who are timid, vacillating, and so afraid of taking a wrong course that they dare not start out to do anything. Those who wait for certainties, who stand on the brink of the stream waiting for somebody to push them in, never reach the other shore.

A great many people seem to have a mortal dread of deciding things. They do not dare to take the responsibility, because they do not know what it may lead to. They are afraid that if they should decide upon one thing today, something better may come up tomorrow and cause them to regret their first decision. These habitual wavers so completely lose their self-confidence that they do not dare to trust themselves to decide anything of importance. Many of them ruin naturally fine minds by nursing the fatal habit of indecision.

There are no two words in the English language that stand out in bolder relief to so great an extent as the words *I will.* There is strength, depth and solidity, decision, confidence and power, determination, courage, vigor and individuality, in the round, ringing tone which characterizes its delivery. It talks to us of triumph over difficulties, of victory in the face of discouragement, of a will to promise and strength to perform, of lofty and daring enterprises, of unfettered aspirations, and of the thousand and one solid impulses by which we master impediments in the way of progress.

Sum and Substance

- When faith in ourselves and in our mission is the dominant note in our lives, nothing can daunt us, no power can keep us from success. Whatever other weaknesses, defects or deficiencies we have, our faith will be a powerful conviction of our ability to perform the things we have undertaken.
- No matter how conspicuous or well defined our talents, unless we exercise them continuously they will deteriorate. Nature's law: "Use or lose," is operative everywhere. There is no getting away from or ignoring it.
- If we recognize the potency of affirmation, of the habit of holding in the mind persistently and affirming that we are what we wish to be and that we can do what we want to do, it would revolutionize our whole lives, it would exempt us

from most of our ills and troubles, and carry us to heights of which we scarcely dream.

- We cannot ever accomplish anything in this world until we affirm in one way or another that we can do what we undertake.
- The worst of all foes to success is sheer, downright laziness.
- Vacillation in making decisions will bring failure or a disappointing result or only a partial success in our endeavors.
- Opposing circumstances create strength. Opposition gives us greater power of resistance. Overcoming one barrier gives us greater ability to overcome the next.
- All doubts and fears, all pessimism and negative thinking poison the very source of life. They sap energy, enthusiasm, ambition, hope, and faith—everything that makes life strong, vital, and creative. Entertain only the mental friends of your ambition, those that will help realize your ideal, that will help to make your dreams come true, to match your vision with reality.
- Humankind was created to do things. Nothing else can take the place of achievement in this life. Real happiness without achievement of some worthy aim is unthinkable.
- The way to learn how to run is to run, the way to learn how to swim is to swim. The way to learn how to develop courage is by the actual exercise of courage in the business of life. By following the examples of great leaders like Lech Walesa, and Richard Branson, we can learn to exercise courage in our endeavors.

8

DEFEATING DEFEAT

We are often afraid of trying new ideas, new ventures, or unusual approaches to solving problems because we are afraid of failure. Fear of failure is a human trait. Nobody wants to suffer the pains of defeat, but no endeavor can succeed unless it is attempted and with every attempt there is the risk that it will not work.

Learn From Your Failures

All of us have failed in many of the things we have tried throughout our lives, but we learn from our mistakes and use what we have learned to overcome them. The first time we try something new, it is likely that we will not succeed. When little Tricia tried to put together her first jigsaw puzzle, she cried in frustration. The parts simply would not fit together.

But with patience and some guidance from her mother, she began to identify patterns and in a short while her failures turned into successes. The first time Johnny faced a pitcher in a baseball game, he just couldn't hit the ball. He struck out over and over again, until he got the knack needed to change misses to hits.

Keep Trying

Even when we have experience and know-how, we cannot always be successful. There will be times when we do fail, but we must not let the concept of failure overwhelm us.

R. H. Macy had to close his first seven stores, but instead of giving up as a "failure," he kept trying and became one of Americas leading retailers. Babe Ruth struck out over 1300 times in his career, but that is forgotten because of his 714 home runs.

Seek the Cause

Thomas Edison never gave up, but perseverance alone is not enough. Each time one of his experiments failed, he studied what caused the failure and kept seeking solutions. It is said that he failed almost 1000 times before developing the filament that made the light bulb work.

It is not just the great geniuses and sports champions who have faced and overcome failures and disappointments. All of us, in our jobs and in our personal lives must expect defeats from time to time and be prepared to defeat them.

Justine was upset. She had been sure that the changes she had recommended would speed up the payroll processing procedure, but to her shock, her changes had slowed it down.

Her boss's criticisms made her feel even more stupid about what she had done. But, rather than give up, she probed to find out what it was that caused the idea to fail. She realized that the concept itself was valid, so the cause had to be in the way it was implemented. By changing the manner in which the clerks were trained in the new procedure, she turned failure into success.

Minimize Risk

All new ideas are risky. If it has not been proven successful in the past, there is a good chance that it may not succeed now. When Paul developed a unique marketing plan for the introduction of a new product his company had developed, he recognized that there were many imponderables that might defeat his objective.

To identify what roadblocks might be encountered, he chose to market the product in three cities before developing the final plans for national distribution. From each test, he was able to learn probable problem areas and work to overcome them. By the time the national marketing campaign started, most of the bugs had been detected and corrected and the chances of success greatly increased.

Seek Alternative Solutions

If the new program Peter developed did not work, and work fast, the company would be in serious difficulties. Peter knew that this idea was good, but it was new and had never been tried. If it failed, there would be no time to evaluate the reasons and make adjustments. It just had to work immediately.

To protect himself and his company in the event of possible problems with the new program, Peter developed an alternative solution, less innovative and unlikely to be as effective as the basic plan, but serve as an interim solution. If the basic plan did not succeed, the problem would at least be under control. Further study could then be made to determine why the plan had not worked and additional steps be taken to enable it to succeed.

Psych Yourself To Succeed

When any plan or concept fails, the persons involved with it are likely to be depressed and some may easily give up. We must expect that failures occur and from time to time we may face defeat.

Andrea was devastated. She was so sure that her suggestions would have solved the situation, but despite all of her efforts, it just didn't do the job. "I'm a failure," she thought. "I'm just not up to this kind of challenge."

If this attitude persisted, not only would Andrea remain unhappy, but it would prevent her from thinking clearly about additional ways to tackle the problem.

We must accept that all of us fail from time to time and that it is not anything to be ashamed of. A self-talk will help remind us that failures are part of trying new things and unless we continue to innovate, we will be become stagnant.

We must remember all of the successes we have had—often after previous failures—and keep telling ourselves that we've done it before and can do it again. Failure is a temporary situation. We have overcome it in the past and we can and will overcome it and succeed again.

Support Staff When They Fail

Managers and supervisors have an added responsibility. They must be willing to deal with failures of their staffs. Of course, there will be times when a subordinate disappoints us by an unsuccessful endeavor. It is tempting to reprimand that person or worse, fire them. Hasty action may cause the loss or demoralization of a potentially good staff member.

A middle manager at IBM made a major misjudgment that cost the company over $100,000. When he was called into the office of Thomas Watson, the man who built IBM into the giant it now is, he expected to be fired. "It was my fault," he told the chairman, "I guess you want my resignation."

"Nonsense," said Watson, "I just invested over $100,000 in your training. Now learn from it and get back to work."

Managers must recognize that if their people are to grow, they must be given opportunities to fail. Otherwise they will fear to take any new, creative, or different approaches.

Getting Performance Back on Track

This does not mean we should ignore failures, errors or poor performance just to maintain the morale of staff members. It is the manager's responsibility to train them to be successful.

In Dale Carnegie Training, participants are taught a six-step approach to getting staff members to speed up their performance.

Step 1 Build common ground

First we should look for ways to build common ground between the person with whom we are working and us. Establish rapport. Rapport is a reservoir of good will and mutual trust accumulated over a long period of fair treatment. When we meet, begin by putting that person at ease and reducing their anxiety. Help him or her feel comfortable. Communicate in an empathetic manner and then conversationally get to the issue at hand.

Step 2 Cushion

Cushion language to avoid abruptness and the potential of placing the individual on defense. Look for a comfortable way to bridge from the conversational rapport building to the issue that needs to be addressed.

Instead of just saying: "that's wrong," cushion your comment by saying something like, "I see that you are on the way to solving this, may I suggest…" then state how improvement can be achieved.

Step 3 Focus on the problem—not the person

During this step, we must focus on the problem and not the person. Eliminate personal pronouns and depersonalize the problem. It was the action that was wrong, not the person who did it. We want to give the other person a chance to explain what happened and then let that person know what we know about the problem. We should listen to understand and to determine whether he or she is accepting responsibility or blaming it on others and avoiding responsibility. The goal is to gather facts and information to be able to accurately identify the problem and its cause. Reduce defensiveness by asking questions and not jumping to conclusions. The different perspectives will surface, and the root cause of the problem should be identified.

Step 4 Explore options together

The purpose of this step is to remedy the problem, to reduce the chance of the mistake happening again, and to restore the person's performance. It also involves planning to devise a way to keep the problem from occurring again. Encourage feedback. This step should be handled differently with the employee who accepts responsibility than with the one who blames and avoids taking responsibility. With the responsible employee, effective questioning, listening, and coaching can be used to encourage him or her to suggest ways to correct the situation. The employee can be involved in a problem analysis and decision-making process and more likely to be committed when they help provide the solution. For the "blaming" or "avoiding" employee, the manager may first need to reaffirm performance expectations and to coach for acceptance of responsibility to restore accountability. Check for understanding and seek to gain consensus.

Step 5 Establish commitment

This step is focused on the person. Obviously a person who has erred feels, to some degree, like a failure and is likely to be less inclined to approach the next opportunity with confidence. Therefore, the manager needs to help the employee see the situation in a different context.

The staff member needs to be reassured of his or her value and importance to the organization and of the manger's support and encouragement. The employee should leave the meeting motivated to achieve optimal performance because he or she perceives a solid relationship with the organization.

The member's commitment to restoring a high performance level and the organization's commitment to the associate's success should be affirmed.

Step 6 Hold accountable

The staff member should leave the meeting with a sense of accountability and an understanding of what the company's expectations are.

Sometimes we find that the employee is not a good fit with a particular task, project, or department. We may need to explore what the employee's strengths, interests, and goals are and search for a better fit within the company for a better match. It is an injustice to employees and companies when we perpetuate a situation where individuals feel that they can never succeed. The last resort after attempts to coach them for desired performance is to remove them from this area of responsibility.

Perseverance and Innovation

All endeavors we undertake cannot succeed. Interspersed with the joy of success is the bitterness of failure. By dealing with failures constructively, we can often turn those failures into successes.

When Lee Iacocca was fired from the Ford Motor Company he was at the lowest point in his career. How he turned this defeat into success in his new job as CEO of Chrysler is well known. In his autobiography, he reported that, immediately upon starting his new job, he was faced with the probability of an even more devastating defeat. Chrysler was on the verge of bankruptcy. A lesser person might have quit right then, rather than moving from one failure to another. But by innovative thinking and perseverance, Iacocca confronted this crisis and defeated it.

Change Direction

Don was more than an ordinary musician. His dream was to be a famous concert violinist. After graduating from the prestigious Juilliard School of Music, he entered several of the major competitions, but never finished in the top group of winners. After all those years of study, he realized that, although he was a competent violinist, he did not have what it takes to reach the top. He could have settled for less and become a member of a symphony orchestra—a job that would give him steady employment and still use his talents. However, Don had the desire to be at the top in his field—not just one of many musicians.

He carefully studied his options and noted a real dearth of knowledgeable musicians in the production end of the recording business. He was hired by a major record company as an Assistant Producer to work in the production of classical records. His talents and knowledge of his field soon led to his promotion—eventually to the head of this department.

Several years later, Don faced another crisis. The Classical Record Department, never a significant moneymaker, was cut back in a cost-saving reorganization. Don was laid off. Again, Don had to change direction. He set himself up as a consulting producer and offered his services to his former employer and other record companies. With his history of achievement in classical record production, he soon became one of the leading independent producers in his field.

On two occasions, Don rather than mourning his failures, turned defeat into success by analyzing his strengths and changing his direction to best use his talents.

Change Goals

When Christine received her last rejection letter from the medical schools to which she had applied, she was distraught. All her life she had planned to be a doctor. In college all of her courses were geared to a medical career. She was a bright student and had expected no problem in being accepted by a medical school. However, her grades in the science courses were lower than was desirable for medical training.

After two days of brooding, Christine realized she had to make some decision as to what to do now. She examined many choices in the medical field including applying to medical schools in foreign countries, getting a job in a medical-related field or repeating the science courses and raising her grades so she could apply again to those schools that had rejected her. None of these options appealed to her. Serious introspection, followed by discussions with friends, parents and advisors, made her realize that her low marks in science courses were not due to lack of capability, but because she had no deep interest in them. Over the years her real interests had changed, but this had not been reflected in her career aspirations.

By rethinking her goals and with the aid of vocational guidance counseling, Christine recognized that she had many talents and opportunities open in several fields. Changing her goals at this point in her life probably saved her from pursuing a career in which she might have been unhappy.

Returning to Past Successes

After many years as one of the top financial analysts in his firm, Joel was promoted to Division Controller. It didn't take Joel long to realize he was over his head in his new job. His strength was working with figures and now much of his work was dealing with people. He supervised a staff of 40 accountants, computer operators and clerks. He spent much of his time at meetings with other managers, personnel from banks and other financial institutions and his own top management. By the end of the first year, he had been talked to and counseled by his boss several times on the lack of performance in his department.

He was on the verge of resigning and looking for another job, when the Corporate Controller visited his division from the home office. "Joel," he said, "you were one of the best financial analysts we had in this company. Your analyses were brilliant. However, in your current job you are not successful. If you are willing to go back to your old job, I think you will be happier and certainly more valuable to the company."

To go backwards is usually looked upon as a defeat. It means admitting we could not succeed in the higher-level position and it is often a blow to one's ego. Yet, history is full of people who were promoted to jobs above their level of competence. People have different strengths and weaknesses. We should be able to accept that we cannot be all things to all people. By returning to his former position, Joel once again can be valuable to his company—and to himself.

Charles Kettering, the creator of the automobile self-starter and many other inventions, sold his company to General

Motors, where he was appointed vice-president in charge of several operations. Kettering was a terrible administrator and the departments he managed did not meet the standards set by the company. Kettering was finally relieved of his managerial duties and left to concentrate on inventions.

Both he and General Motors benefited because he could now work exclusively in the areas where he was at his best.

Failures and defeats should not lead to depression and mourning. Analyze the reason for the defeat and determine how you can change it into a successful endeavor.

> *Develop success from failures. Discouragement and failure are two of the surest stepping stones to success.*
>
> *Dale Carnegie*

Overcoming Disappointment on the Job

When Victor joined his company, he set as his goal to be the branch manager within five years. Four years later he isn't even close to reaching his goal. He feels unhappy, letdown and demotivated. His thoughts vary from dreaming of a sudden change in his fortunes to bemoaning his ill luck.

Why hasn't Victor met his goal? Perhaps it is due to circumstances being beyond his control such as a recession or a tough competitive situation. Or perhaps Victor has not demonstrated his best capabilities in the assignments given to him. If the former, Victor may have to set new goals or seek a new job where circumstances are more favorable.

Promotions Must Be Earned

However, the reason for one's failure to move up in the company may not be due to outside factors. It may be that Victor had not earned the expected promotion. Just putting in one's time is not enough. Victor should reevaluate his work, discuss with his supervisor how he can improve, and take additional training to prepare himself for advancement of his position.

Meredith was very upset. Her boss had retired and she expected that she would be promoted to her job. After all, she was the most senior person in the department and her work was always good. Not only did she not get the promotion, but the company brought in an outsider who knew nothing about the department—"It just wasn't fair."

Well, why didn't Meredith get her boss's job? When a company chooses a person for a leadership position, it is certainly going to consider a person's work record, reliability and competence, but it also must seek people with the characteristics that show that they have more than just technical competence. They must have those special ingredients that make them stand out. They must be people who have shown they are willing to stretch to do more than just the routine job.

Stretch

Jack, the executive vice-president, was meeting with Leo, a middle level manager who was about to retire. After they completed their discussion of the transition of Leo's work to his successor, Leo said: "Jack, there's something that has been on my mind a long time. It has bothered and frustrated me for years, but were I not retiring, I wouldn't have dared ask you. You and I started in this company at approximately the same time. You're the executive vice-president and I have never risen above the middle level of management. Where did I go wrong? I have done excellent work. My bosses have always given me excellent reviews. I've always done everything I have been asked to do and did it well. What did you do that I failed to do that put you so far ahead of where I am?"

"Leo, you just answered your own question. You always did everything you were asked to do, but that was all you did. I got where I am because I reached out to do more than what I had to do in my regular work. I volunteered to take on assignments nobody else wanted. I initiated ideas and sold these ideas to top management. Sure I took risks, because some of them may not have worked and cost the company money—and some of them did fail, but overall I made myself invaluable to the company. When I felt I had done all I could in the department where I was assigned, I asked for transfer to another department where I could learn more about the company and contribute in added ways. Doing one's job well is important, and is the basis for all else, but it is doing more than what one has to do that brings one to the attention of the top managers who decide who moves up."

Too many people are like Leo and Meredith and perhaps, Victor. They do good work and expect that is enough. It is important, but as Jack said, one has to stretch to really get ahead.

Understanding Why

If you are being by-passed while others are being promoted, think carefully what you can do to earn the right to be considered for the next opportunity. Answer these ten questions:

1. How can I make my current work more valuable to the company?
2. What can I do for this company that I am not doing?
3. In what ways can I improve how things are done in my department?
4. What new and different aspects of the work could I learn so I can be more valuable to this organization?
5. What steps might I take to let my bosses know I am willing to accept more responsibility?
6. What can I learn about what other departments are doing that might fit into my goals?
7. If I have gone as far as I can in my current job, are there other jobs within the organization I can do?
8. Are there assignments other people are reluctant to do that I might volunteer to perform?
9. How can I improve my accomplishments as a manager by getting my people to be better performers?
10. Am I willing to make the commitment and undergo the sacrifices and take necessary risks to earn the right to move up the management ladder?

Be the Master of Your Own Fate

Don't blame your frustrations on the system—unless it truly is the system. If an honest evaluation of why you are not reaching your goals shows that you can do something to overcome what is holding you back, identify what it is you are not currently doing and correct it. By taking overt steps to become an outstanding employee, not just a good worker, you will put yourself on the road to success.

> *We can all endure disaster and tragedy, and triumph over them—if we have to. We may not think we can, but we have surprisingly strong inner resources that will see us through if we will only make use of them. We are stronger than we think.*
>
> *Dale Carnegie*

Bouncing Back

It is not uncommon for a major disappointment, whether in business or in other aspects of one's life, to cause one's morale to plummet and to engender a grave blow to one's self-confidence. Unless corrective action is taken immediately, this may deteriorate into self-pity, failure, and unhappiness.

"I don't think I'll ever recover from the loss of this account." Clyde thought. He was deeply depressed. For several years his largest customer, the Lincoln Manufacturing Company, had accounted for 30 percent of his income. He had just learned that the company was going to close its plant in Toledo and consolidate its operations with their Houston facility.

For the next few weeks Clyde moped about bemoaning his loss. His sales manager gave him pep talks, encouraged him to try develop new accounts, gave him additional leads—but nothing seemed to help.

He called on the prospects, but his presentations were mediocre, his doubts about his abilities seeped through to the customer and he didn't make the sale.

These failures added to the original loss made the situation even worse. Clyde went into a state of deep gloom and seriously considered getting out of selling and seeking a less demanding career.

Set Realistic and Attainable Goals

Clyde had fought hard to become a successful salesman. It would be wrong to let all those good years go down the drain. With the help of his sales manager, he worked his way through the "mourning" stages that follows a serious loss. He finally accepted the fact that the loss of the customer had nothing to do with his competency. He still had the same capability and drive that had enabled him to sell to Lincoln and all his other customers over the years. He had to start afresh with renewed confidence and enthusiasm. The only way to obtain this confidence was by successful selling. He set new goals for himself and discussed them with his manager.

"Art, I'm going to replace that business in six months."

"Fine, Clyde, what is your plan of action?"

"I'll work, really work long and hard and I'll make it."

"I'm glad you feel this way, but let's study the market and set realistic goals. If you set too high a goal in too short a time, you are likely not to make it. It is more important for you to set lower goals that you are sure to reach and then work up from there."

Art was right. The best way to bounce back is to experience new successes. If the initial goals are too high, this is less likely to occur. By setting realistic and attainable goals, each time we reach a goal, we are adding credibility to the image we have of ourselves.

We are giving ourselves proof of our capability and this builds a solid foundation for our next step. Success breeds success and by following Art's advice, Clyde was not only able to replace his lost business but also increase his total sales over the next several months.

Focus on Past Achievements

Marybeth's marriage had been a disaster. Her ex-husband's constant berating had turned a vibrant, self-assured woman into a frightened, despondent defeatist. She had married just after her college graduation and although she wanted to teach, her husband persuaded her to take a clerical job in a bank. She felt she could do better, but he kept telling her she was not capable of any position of responsibility. He found fault with everything she did and inflated his ego by debasing her. After three years of this, she divorced him and tried to build her life anew.

She reviewed her past and realized that she was happiest and most successful when she was in college. She enrolled in the continuing education division of a local college. Her class participation, research reports, and excellent grades reinforced her image of herself as an achiever. This gave her the courage to apply for matriculation in a Master's degree program, where she did so well that she was asked to join the faculty when she attains her degree.

By focusing on past achievements and seeking opportunity to repeat them, Marybeth pulled herself out of her dejection and bounced back to a happy and satisfying life.

Convert "Worry" to "Concern"

Carlos couldn't sleep. He was worried sick. In a week his new boss would take over—a stranger. He had gotten along famously with his old boss, but when he retired, instead of appointing one of the old-timers to the supervisor's job, they hired an outsider. "Maybe this new guy would be too tough; maybe he won't like me."

For the next few days he was nervous on the job and had great difficulty sleeping. He noticed that his friend and co-worker, Tony, didn't seem to be upset, so he asked him: "Tony, aren't you worried about the new boss?"

Tony shook his head. "Sure, I'm concerned. He could make changes here. But I'm not worried. What is the worst thing that can happen? Well the worst is he could fire me.

If he fires me, I have acquired good skills here so I'd just get another job. However, there is no real reason he should fire me. I've done a good job and will continue to do so. If he makes changes, I can live with them—and if I can't, there are other jobs around. So why worry?"

Carlos took this to heart and was able to work without worry and not lose more sleep. Sure, he would be concerned, but by keeping these precepts on controlling worry, he was able to handle this situation with assurance.

Beating the Blues

All of us have within ourselves the capability of bouncing back and beating those blues that get us down when things go wrong. We can work to correct the tangible problems, but we also have to make overt efforts to overcome the psychological depression that may sap our strengths and energy.

When the *blues* hit, we must not let it dim our hope. The bright *orange* sun is still there. It is only hidden temporarily behind the *ebony* clouds. The path to those *silver* linings may be barred by *green* envy of others, distorted by *purple* rage or impeded by *yellow* lights that may make us overcautious. To get back into the *pink*, we must visualize our goals with *crystal* clarity and fan those *red* flames of our zeal to overcome our problems to a *white* heat of strength and determination that will enable us to leap over the *black* pits that block us from our goals and change the color of our lives from dark *gray* to glittering *gold*.

Sum and Substance

- All endeavors we undertake cannot succeed. Interspersed with the joy of success is the bitterness of failure. By dealing with failures constructively, we can often turn those failures into successes.
- We must expect that failures occur from time to time and condition ourselves not to let it depress us.
- If we are managers, it is our responsibility to encourage our staffs when they fail and train them to be successful.
- To succeed, good performance is not enough. To really get ahead, we must perform over and above what is expected of us, innovate and have the courage to take risks that may not work out.

- To cultivate a mental attitude that will bring peace and happiness, Dale Carnegie advices that we should:
  1. Fill our minds with thoughts of peace, courage, health and hope.
  2. Never try to get even with our enemies.
  3. Expect ingratitude.
  4. Count our blessings—not our troubles.
  5. Do not imitate others.
  6. Try to profit from our losses.
  7. Create happiness for others.

Appendix A

ABOUT DALE CARNEGIE & ASSOCIATES, INC.

Founded in 1912, Dale Carnegie Training has evolved from one man's belief in the power of self-improvement to a performance-based training company with offices worldwide. It focuses on giving people in business the opportunity to sharpen their skills and improve their performance in order to build positive, steady, and profitable results.

Dale Carnegie's original body of knowledge has been constantly updated, expanded and refined through nearly a century's worth of real-life business experiences. The 160 Dale Carnegie Franchisees around the world use their training and consulting services with companies of all sizes in all business segments to increase knowledge and performance. The result of this collective, global experience is an expanding reservoir of business acumen that our clients rely on to drive business results.

Headquartered in Hauppauge, New York, Dale Carnegie Training is represented in all 50 of the United States and over 75 countries. More than 2,700 instructors present Dale Carnegie Training programs in more than 25 languages. Dale Carnegie Training is dedicated to serving the business community worldwide. In fact, approximately 7 million people have completed Dale Carnegie Training.

Dale Carnegie Training emphasizes practical principles and processes by designing programs that offer people the knowledge, skills and practices they need to add value to their businesses. Connecting proven solutions with real-world challenges, Dale Carnegie Training is recognized internationally as the leader in bringing out the best in people.

Among the graduates of these programs are CEOs of major corporations, owners and managers of businesses of every size and every commercial and industrial activity, legislative and executive leaders of governments and countless individuals whose lives have been enriched by the experience.

In an ongoing global survey on customer satisfaction, 99 percent of Dale Carnegie Training graduates express satisfaction with the training they receive.

Appendix B

DALE CARNEGIE'S PRINCIPLES

Become a friendlier person

1. Don't criticize, condemn or complain.
2. Give honest, sincere appreciation.
3. Arouse in the other person an eager want.
4. Become genuinely interested in other people.
5. Smile.
6. Remember that a person's name is to that person the sweetest sound in any language.
7. Be a good listener. Encourage others to talk about themselves.
8. Talk in terms of the other person's interests.
9. Make the other person feel important—and do it sincerely.
10. To get the best of an argument—avoid it.
11. Show respect for the other person's opinion. Never tell a person he or she is wrong.

12. If you are wrong, admit it quickly, emphatically.
13. Begin in a friendly way.
14. Get the other person to say "yes" immediately.
15. Let the other person do a great deal of the talking.
16. Let the other person feel the idea is his or hers.
17. Try honestly to see things from the other person's point of view.
18. Be sympathetic with the other person's ideas and desires.
19. Appeal to the nobler motives.
20. Dramatize your ideas.
21. Throw down a challenge.
22. Begin with praise and honest appreciation.
23. Call attention to people's mistakes indirectly.
24. Talk about your own mistakes before criticizing the other person.
25. Ask questions instead of giving direct orders.
26. Let the other person save face.
27. Praise the slightest improvement. Be "hearty in your approbation and lavish in your praise."
28. Give the other person a fine reputation to live up to.
29. Use encouragement. Make the fault seem easy to correct.
30. Make the other person happy about doing the thing you suggest.

Fundamental Principles for Overcoming Worry

1. Live in "day-tight compartments."
2. How to face trouble:
   Ask yourself: "What is the worst that can possibly happen?"
3. Prepare to accept the worst.
4. Try to improve on the worst.

5. Remind yourself of the exorbitant price you can pay for worry in terms of your health.

Basic Techniques in Analyzing Worry

1. Get all the facts.
2. Weigh all the facts—then come to a decision.
3. Once a decision is reached—act!
4. Write out and answer the following questions:
   - What is the problem?
   - What are the causes of the problem?
   - What are the possible solutions?
   - What is the best possible solution?
5. Break the habit of worrying before it breaks you.
6. Keep busy.
7. Don't fuss about trifles.
8. Use the law of averages to outlaw your worries.
9. Cooperate with the inevitable.
10. Decide just how much anxiety a thing may be worth and refuse to give it more.
11. Don't worry about the past.
12. Cultivate a mental attitude that will bring you peace and happiness.
13. Fill your mind with thoughts of peace, courage, health and hope.
14. Never try to get even with your enemies.
15. Expect ingratitude.
16. Count your blessings—not your troubles.
17. Do not imitate others.
18. Try to profit from your losses.
19. Create happiness for others.